ISAAC BUTTERFIELD
BETTER MAN

**For my son Atticus
and wife Clare,
You are everything . . .**

Copyright © 2024 Isaac Butterfield

All rights reserved. The author asserts their moral rights in this work throughout the world without waiver. No part of this book may be reproduced, or stored in a retrieval system, or transmitted in any form or by any means, electronic, mechanical, photocopying, recording, or otherwise, without express written permission of the publisher. For information about permission to reproduce selections from this book, contact publishing@rabbitgroup.com

ISBN 9781761285554 (print)

Published by:

Rabbit Group LLC
New York, New York, 10013

Printed in China

Foreword by Friendly Jordies vii

How to read a book xiii

Chapter 1: Rock bottom 1

Chapter 2: Catacombs 15

Chapter 3: 33.3 per cent 23

Chapter 4: Cancelled 37

Chapter 5: Decisively engaged 59

Chapter 6: So you're going to be a dad 75

Chapter 7: Small wins 93

Chapter 8: Marry your best friend 107

Chapter 9: Free speech 125

Chapter 10: Be careful of new religions 143

Chapter 11: You are weak 149

Chapter 12: Mansplaining men 167

Chapter 13: It's okay to be masculine 185

Chapter 14: Do things you hate 201

Foreword

If you ask anyone in the Australian comedy scene (who isn't an insufferable narcissist — so minus 80% of the Australian comedy scene) what they think of Isaac Butterfield, the response will invariably be something like, "He's the kindest man in the business . . . and yet he's at the epicentre of *every* controversy."

It's a curious paradox, one that is frequently discussed in green rooms across the country. I think this book will put an end to the chin-scratching. This book answers that paradox. The answer is confronting. It should have never been a paradox to begin with.

It's hard to believe now, but the Australian comedy scene used to routinely spawn pioneering, world-class performers. Ali G? Norman Gunston did it decades ago. Whenever Dave Chapelle refers to himself as the G.O.A.T. I wince. Not just at the gall of it, but also because he's not Rodney Rude's arsehole.

Even if you look at that oh-so-hated Melburnian brand of "wanker" comedy; there was a time when our cultural capital was belting out scholarly, finely tuned, virtuosos. Melbourne had more rustic versions of the comedic institutions that Japan boasts. They brewed the likes of Lano & Woodley, masters of slapstick and the absurd. And Greg Fleet, a brilliant raconteur whose observational wit was undeniable and greatly paired with his theatrical prowess. In short, Australian comedy had its golden age. Isaac Butterfield and his contemporaries were not fortunate enough to bask in it.

Monopolisation of Australian media led to an insipid hollowing out of the infrastructure that built these unique talents. What remained of the bones were tossed to undeserving wallies of the upper class — evil cowards who have no business in comedy. Rightfully, they should be the targets of it. Not because that would be "punching up"; purely because they're annoying cunts. A generation of grizzled greats was replaced with a generation of frightened prep schoolers whose limp performances in front of ever-dwindling crowds are little more than auditions for *The Project*, and so severely lacking in the basic tools of their craft that they seem oblivious to the irony that, "If one was on television but no one was around to watch it . . ."

If that economic reality weren't stark enough, around 2014 an alien fog of American corporate ideology seeped its way over the Pacific and was gleefully huffed by the native cultural elite. One of its key criteria was to smash the ancient pillars of comedy, those pillars that have been observed as far back as Aristotle: the puerile; the shocking; the stereotypical.

These foundations were carelessly tossed aside and without warning replaced with a vain attempt to reengineer an art form that is at its core a celebration of the vile. The puerile was replaced with tantrums. The shocking with haughty lectures. Stereotypes with virtue signalling. This was the epoch in which Isaac was forged. Despise him as they might, he is to them what his YouTube channel is to his fans; a react.

Aren't we all shaped by the historical context of our time? If Australian comedy was the Roman Empire we would be trudging through the era of Constantine, not Augustus. The grand project we inherited cannot flourish; in our age it must fight merely to exist and Isaac, thankfully, is at the vanguard of that fight, pitching gruelling battles on ever-shrinking territory. The licence to offend that comedians were once afforded as a given . . . has been revoked. Thus, Isaac's absurd raison d'être was cast. An endless, impassioned monologue pleading for that licence to be renewed. As a fellow traveller I have often thought, *Thank god he's taking the slings and arrows in this struggle. Imagine if he wasn't?* Surely someone else would have picked up the mantle; after all, it's a global war and the allure of fame is an enticing siren. The question, though, is would they have had Isaac's heart?

The world's firebrands are but echoes of the Western Front in World War I. Each nation has a particular fighting style. The British with their pompous sterility. The Americans with their aggressive, unsubtle brashness. If you want to see this cultural disconnect, watch Isaac on the *Whatever Podcast*. What a lamentation! How differently this war would have been waged had an Australian general been at the helm. Instead of offence igniting offence in a self-perpetuating firestorm it could have been stoked to an ember that warmed us all with this nation's weapon of choice: well-natured, jocular bantz. Isaac showed us that the war could have been fought, if I dare be so aggrandising, in a spirit befitting the Anzacs, as it is *indeed* the spirit of the Anzacs — larrikinism. My spellcheck doesn't even recognise the word, which reveals how unique this character is to us as a people. A rowdy, uncultivated youth. A shit stirrer grounded by a good heart and a solemn reverence for mateship. The larrikin is an archetype that will rouse a knowing smile out of any Australian. It's the epitome of us as a people — dickheads with hearts of gold.

This is why we used to punch well above our weight in comedy. Comedy comes to Australians as naturally as soccer comes to Brazilians and rowing to Venetians. It's in our blood to take the piss. We know we're joking because joking is all we know.

Witnessing Isaac in America, you realise that if he weren't adding these uniquely Australian spices to that foreign shit soup it would have hit the fan anyway. These hot button issues would have seared through our iPhones — the only filter available would have been the American flag. We would have been angrier and meaner, we needed a larrikin to translate it into Australiana, and by doing so Isaac was doing what all good Australians do in a wildfire. You back burn. He channelled the fire into fuelling the eternal flame for another generation and thus ensured that larrikinism flickered away through the comedic dark ages. It is for this reason that I think he should be regarded as one of the Australian greats. But in the age of rust.

It is often noted that in times of decline people forget

what was taken for granted in the golden age. In the golden age, what Isaac is doing wasn't regarded as "offensive". It used to be well understood that you can be Dr Jekyll in your personal life and Mr Hyde on stage. In fact, you *should* be. It's a perfectly natural place for both. It seems both disturbing and stupid that the "Isaac paradox" is so misunderstood by comedians across the country as it used to go by a different name; "being an Australian man". That's why this book needed to be written.

It was while I was reading it that I was struck with the sad realisation that for centuries, British men have been handed a gentlemen's guide. It's a rite of passage that has served both men and the culture well. The Australian equivalent should have been a larrikin's guide. There is great need for a refinement and reverence of this archetype that has not only served this nation well but animated its destiny. Isaac has written such a guide and he was exactly the right man for it. I am therefore humbled to welcome you good motherfuckers to Isaac Butterfield's *Better Man*. Peace in the Middle East.

Jordan Shanks "Friendly Jordies"

How to read a book

GROWING UP, I wasn't the biggest reader. In fact, I didn't read my first book until I was in my twenties. But when I did, I was hooked. Reading has a power far beyond that of audiobooks and videos; it almost feels like you are having a lived experience through reading the words on the page. The author's story becomes your story for that brief moment in your day when your head is buried in a book.

Ever since I started touring around Australia and the world, people have come up to me at each show and divulged that I'm the first comedian they have ever seen live. I love hearing this and I always respond with the question, "Would you come back?" They usually answer, "Yes, of course. What a great show. You are the comedy messiah." But if they ever dare to say, "No, I didn't really enjoy the show," then I know they're talking pure bullshit because they have never seen a show before, so why the fuck would I listen to them?

But it got me thinking, *If so many people are seeing comedy for the first time because of me — and the power of the internet — then maybe the trend would continue into a book . . .* For some, this may very well be the first book they have ever read. It might seem unnecessary, but here is a guide for you book virgins on how to read a book.

You may or may not know this, but there are many books out there. Millions. Crazy, right?

Now you could have chosen *The Catcher in the Rye*, *To Kill a Mockingbird* or even *1984*. All classics you've probably heard of, but instead you chose my book.

And now that we have covered your first mistake, let me tell you why book choice matters. Personally, I don't like fiction, just not a fan. I prefer to read someone's thoughts about the world or a particular subject. I prefer autobiographies, books on society and culture, books on psychology — that's my jam. When it comes to having to use my imagination to create worlds and characters, my brain just isn't as capable as the creatives who work for the big movie studios. So I'm sorry. Give me *The Lord of the Rings* movie over the books any day.

But everyone's different. So choose a book that is palatable and digestible to start you off. Don't go balls deep — invest in something that will pique your interest but not something that's overly complicated. Start your life of reading with a simple text, a text for dummies; this book.

Better Man is designed in a very particular way; the topics are relatable for everyone. It's not an overly long book, and

I didn't buy a thesaurus to impress you with words I can't pronounce. What I have done is structured each chapter with what most people feel comfortable reading in a single sitting. Most of the chapters can be covered in less than 30 minutes. And most can be read one at a time without you losing your place. In a world where attention spans are shrinking by the second and people challenge each other to read 10 pages a day like it's no mean feat, I felt if I made the chapters too long I'd lose some of you, and if I made them too short I wouldn't be able to get out the story I want to tell. *This book*, I feel, is in the "Goldilocks zone": not too big, not too little, just right. So whether you're a first-time reader or a seasoned veteran, whoever you are and wherever you come from, this book is for you.

Once you start a chapter, read it till the end, then come back and finish the next, if you're that way inclined. There is no right or wrong way to consume these pages, just do your thing, but actually *do* it. Set yourself a goal. Books can be difficult for those of us who aren't avid readers. Setting a goal of a chapter a day is still difficult enough to fill you with pride when you achieve the prize of turning that final page, but also it allows you to have some anticipation of what you will read tomorrow. It's my hope that you will look forward to each new chapter.

Like running, weightlifting, studying, or learning any new skill, reading is all about reps; the more you do, the better you become. The first time you do it you may hate it, but over time it may or may not become your jam. If it does become something that excites you, wonderful, if not then just finish my fucking book, thanks.

In anticipation of the marvellous feeling you will have finishing each chapter of this fine work of literary art, please enjoy the dopamine release you feel from being able to

Turn

This

Page

Like

You

Have

Actually

Achieved

Something

You

Are

Welcome.

BETTER
MAN

Chapter 1: **Rock bottom**

OPENED IN 1971 by Robert Askin, the then Premier of New South Wales, the bridge was second only in size to the Sydney Harbour Bridge. It resembled it too, if you removed all the bells, whistles, charm, elegance, and the fact that no one in their right mind would mistake this bridge for the one synonymous with Australia. It actually made architects, or anyone who even gives a slight fuck about design or style, cry themselves to sleep at night. It definitely isn't on any postcards, no artists have ever or would ever paint it; it's nothing but a section of an unremarkable road crossing a section of unremarkable river.

It is a steep bridge, I'll give it that. You almost feel like your car won't make it the whole way up sometimes — and who knows what's on the other side. In my early teenage years

I was driving with my father once and his car lost all power going up the bridge and only just crawled over the apex.

The bridge may have been a feat of engineering for its time — and I suppose it's handy for those who live nearby or use it on a regular basis — but it's gross, for all intents and purposes. It's a shit bridge. Nevertheless, this overpass that connects my home town of Newcastle to its airport and surrounding areas would serve as a signal for me, almost like a shaman leading me into the very catacombs that were my mind at the time. A beacon that something was wrong, and I was to listen to that bridge whether I liked it or not.

I was at my absolute lowest. There was no further down, any lower and you'd hit granite. The feelings I had were much like the earth's crust, the lower I went the more intense the heat became. The pressure increased daily, eventually becoming so immense I am positive that no one has been there before me. Surely no one could deal with these feelings, the pain, the horror, the internal anguish. (FYI this book becomes lighthearted soon. It's not just me whingeing; I'm setting the scene as it were, so keep reading.)

Anyway, back to the bridge. The name given to the shit bridge is the Stockton Bridge, a four-lane concrete overpass a kilometre in length and 30 metres high at its pinnacle. It really is a ghastly concrete eyesore. The area surrounding it is quite the opposite; the ocean, the sand, the beautiful bush — all magnificent in their own ways, a testament to the gorgeous surroundings we are so lucky to have in our wide brown land.

But it was the top of the bridge, that was the place I couldn't stop thinking about; and the thoughts were intrusive, violent and tragic. They came from the ether and became reality in almost an instant. Regardless of how hard I tried, with all the might I attempted to muster, I could not for the life of me stop them.

I've learnt as I have gotten older and dealt with my issues, that intrusive thoughts *can't* be stopped and are relatively normal. For example, try this out for size: *don't* think about the Queen and Prince Philip 69ing in Buckingham Palace, absolutely going at it — I mean, when they were alive. Fuck, you see, intrusive thoughts come, they hit you and then they go.

But I didn't know any of that yet.

My intrusive thought was something I obsessed over and it was this: me atop the bridge, leaping to my demise, stopping the pain that was sealed in the front of my brain. I just couldn't shake it. As much as I hate to admit it even now, at the age of 25 I couldn't stop thinking about killing myself. I don't think I ever really wanted to, but the thoughts were unstoppable. It's fucking horrible to write that down but it's the truth and it's a lot of peoples' truths. And that's partly why I'm writing this book; to list my thoughts, my failures and my success; and to give you hope that there *is* light at the end of the tunnel — motivation, a laugh and a friend.

But back when I was 25, I was dealing with something people laugh and joke about on a daily basis, something that people confuse with being nervous. I was suffering from anxiety — generalised anxiety disorder to be precise — and eventually full-blown panic attacks.

—

Mental illness is thriving like never before. It almost seems popular, undermining the psychological fortitude of so many of us like termites. But why? Is it social media? An individual's upbringing? Their relationships? Work? Bullying? What?

I know many people claim to be anxious but there is a very big difference between feeling anxious and having generalised anxiety disorder. If you are anxious you feel worried, nervous or scared. If you have something coming up you are uneasy about, it almost makes sense how your body is acting. But when you are dealing with the real deal, your body is *constantly* and *completely* shutting down. You aren't yourself, your reptile brain has taken full control and acts like there is immediate danger surrounding you. When you are dealing with these issues, the body thinks it's about to be attacked by a lion, when in reality there is no danger at all. That's how I explain it to people. You are sitting on the lounge watching TV but your body is in the fight and flight mode as if a fucking grizzly bear is sitting next to you.

I've never had depression so can't comment on that, but I don't think people understand quite how debilitating disorders like the panic and anxiety disorder I was diagnosed with can be. We all deal with anxiety, but I feel it can be grouped into three categories:

Category 1: You are nervous about something coming up, you have to do a speech at school or a wedding, something most of us can relate to. It is a worry not so much a fear. This kind of anxiety often disappears the moment the stressor is gone. You finish your speech, you have no reason to worry anymore and life goes on. This is the natural level of anxiety that 99 per cent of people live through and if you don't have this experience with at least one or two things in life you are probably a pathetic psycho who skins cats for fun.

Category 2: Generalised anxiety disorder (GAD). This is where I lived and still live intermittently. Some days were better than others but more often than not I would, from the moment I woke up to the moment I went to sleep, be in a constant state of panic. This category is a "spectrum" and most people experience this terrifying state of mind once or twice a day, or sometimes once a week. For some, like me, it was non-stop.

I found that with treatment, I went from feeling like this every waking hour to, slowly but surely, only 12 hours a day, then eventually it was only for a few hours and now, four or five years later, it's maybe a few hours a week.

Category 3: Agoraphobia. I personally cannot speak too much on the worst category of anxiety, but people with agoraphobia are unable to leave the house. I can only imagine the internal hell they deal with and my heart goes out to them, it really does. I do hope they keep fighting and find solace in the fact they are not alone and many others have walked in their shoes and gone on to not only beat this horrifying mental illness but thrive in the real world.

So I guess the question becomes why?

It's hard to say. For me, I've always had it. I panicked easily when I was a kid, I was terrified of new experiences and if Mum was five minutes late picking me up from school, I immediately assumed she was dead and I would break down in tears. As I got older, it got worse. In Year 9 I had three months off school. Every day when I walked to the bus stop a mere 50 metres from my house, I felt physically ill. I thought I was about to vomit every single morning. I couldn't get on the bus. I would stand near the bus stop watching my bus go past, dry heaving. I physically could not get on that bus.

I went to the doctor after a few weeks of this and explained the situation. He asked if I was anxious.

"No," I said and thus ended his investigation into anxiety. It must be something else.

So I was prescribed Nexium, which is used to treat gastroesophageal reflux disease and peptic ulcers and that was that. But I still had the problem a few weeks later, so the doctor decided to stick a camera up my arse and down my throat. He cleaned it between insertions. But still no answers, oh well.

In the end, the solution to treating my anxiety was "exposure therapy". My mum and dad forced me into the car and made me go to school. Within a few weeks it was gone.

—

When I was 20 I began to experience events that would lead me to looking at the Stockton Bridge as the answer to my problems and the only way out.

I was staying with my grandparents at the time, who I love dearly, in a single bed — living the dream! One night I rolled to my right side and felt this strange movement in my eyes; an uncontrollable change in where I was looking, almost as uncontrollable as shutting your eyes when you sneeze. My left eye, independently of the right, began trying to look at something behind me. It continued until my eye couldn't turn any more, then my neck followed, all of this uncontrollable, like I was trying to see behind myself. My neck, my head, my eyes, everything locked in that position. I was panicking. *What the fuck is going on? Do I call out for help?* Then as quickly as it began it was over. Maybe 10 seconds and I was back to normal. I was pretty shaken by the experience, and I really didn't know what to do or think.

In a period of six weeks I experienced about 10 of these episodes, but only ever when I was in bed, so it wasn't really too much of an issue. Until, that is, I was about 21 and it started happening while playing football. I played rugby league for 17 years from the age of six. It was in my family, my dad was a professional rugby league player and honestly in the early part of my life, it's all I wanted to be — until I found comedy.

Unfortunately these issues with my head and neck started affecting me whilst playing. I would run the ball into the opposition, have a big collision and from the whiplash I would fall into one of these "fits". It was embarrassing to say the least, but I could usually fob it off as a head knock or minor concussion. I'd just stay on the ground and wait until it was over, then get to my feet and the other players and the crowd would be none the wiser.

That happened maybe three times the first year, more after that. During one game against Newcastle University, we needed a big play, so I sprinted out of the defensive line at one of the oncoming 100 kilogram front rowers. I hit him with one of the best shoulder charges you have even seen. He went down and was out cold. The tiny crowd went wild. A big moment, a turn in the game, and then *I* hit the deck because I had a fit. The thing about these fits is that I'm completely conscious throughout, and can actually stand up while they happen. It's easier to lie down because when your head turns you are like a dog trying to catch its tail — you end up just spinning in circles. But this time something else happened; I went blind in my left eye. For 10 to 15 seconds it was like someone had taken the eyeball from my skull. Goes without saying I was terrified.

During another game I took the run of the kick off, ran into the defensive line, KO'ed the opposite front rower and looked like a hero, until I collapsed and started having a fit.

Then, the night after my 21st birthday party at the Gunyah Hotel, where I used to work, I was carrying the leftover birthday cake from the night before and I had one standing on the stairs. At this point I thought to myself, *Okay, I need to see the doctor again.*

So on the 14th of July 2014, my actual 21st birthday, I went to the doctor's alone. I didn't tell anyone I was going. I walked in with fear but without a sense of what I was actually walking into. In reality I was walking into a diagnosis that would sit with me for the rest of my life. I explained my symptoms, and was met with a doctor googling — which, let's face it, is never a good sign. Eventually, he explained that what he *thought* I may be facing.

"You know those people in wheelchairs who are stuck in a position and they can't move?"

"You think I have that, doc?"

"Maybe. Well, I'm not sure, but you should get an MRI."

Well fuck, mate, you better be sure because right now I've just learnt that my life as I know it — my hopes, my dreams, my expectations for the future — are all over, done, terminated. The thought of me in a wheelchair unable to move angered me. Combine that with the knowledge of the symptoms and a slight understanding of how disastrous neurological conditions can be, I was also scared.

I held my resentment about the news and fury at the doctor close to my chest, thanked him for his time and booked an appointment with a neurologist. That drive home was as lonely as can be, the sheer weight of it was unbearable.

One thing I wonder about now is why didn't I tell my then girlfriend or any of my family earlier? I was all alone and that 15-minute drive felt like an age. It was one of those drives where you are almost at your destination but you forget you've even been driving. When I got home, I went inside, said hello to my family, and told my parents about the visit to the doctor's and what he'd said. I don't really think they understood. I wasn't met with pity or comfort which maybe is a good thing, at least for the pity part. I had my dinner that night surrounded by my family and acted like nothing worried me but inside, my mind, my subconscious, was like a worm on hot pavement, panicking and desperate for salvation.

My entire life had been turned on its head – it felt like my life was over – but the worst part was I didn't have a definitive answer as to what was wrong, I just had guesses, guesses that made my anxiety worse.

—

Perhaps the shittiest part about going to a specialist like a neurologist is the wait times. It's ridiculous. Four months I believe it took for me get in — and when the "medical professional" you see regularly has given you news which means you are basically fucked, that four months feels like a lifetime.

For a few days I was upset, but the anger, sadness and almost grief subsided. Pretty quickly I changed my outlook and decided that if I was going to be in this terrible situation, I may as well make the most of whatever life I had left. I should do the things I'd been meaning to do, take on what I'd been too scared to attempt, and achieve what I had only dreamt of achieving.

Not too long after this, I performed stand-up for the very first time.

What's so crazy about all of this, is that the antagonist in my story is an illness and without that diagnosis, you wouldn't be reading this book. It's funny how you can reach rock bottom and even there you can find motivation, happiness and eventually success. In fact, I think it may be necessary.

—

I'll dive deeper into my stand-up career later, but I felt like the beginning of this book should allow everyone to see with complete transparency that we are all fucked up, our lives are all messes and only some of us choose to make a change.

In the months leading up to my next appointment with the specialist I had my first MRI. I've had a few since but none compare to sliding into that tube for the very first time; claustrophobia doesn't do it justice. My eyes were darting back and forth, I was on the edge of a fit for 45 minutes. I was fighting but barely holding on. I couldn't allow the fit to happen. If I did, the image would be ruined and I'd have to start again. I gritted my teeth and held on for dear life and eventually came out the other side. But, can I just say, fuck MRIs.

In the next few months I had a few more fits, the most notable of which was in the surf at Coogee Beach after a big night on the beers at a family wedding. It was a massive night. I was staying in a room with three of my brothers, Jonas, Darcy and Fintan, who were all under 12 at this point. I came back to the hotel with my dad well after midnight and then proceeded to spew into the toilet with my baby brothers checking in on me, one of my finest moments.

In the morning I was woken by Jonas, the middle brother. He was crying, screaming, he was such a sook. Growing up you have no idea. He ran to Mum and told her that I had pissed all over his iPod and in his bag — to make matters worse, I had. This was how blind drunk I was; I pissed all over the hotel room and I was so embarrassed when Mum came in. I pleaded with her. "I'm so sorry, Mum." She had the shits, she yelled, "Isaac, you're just like your bloody father, he pissed the bed too!"

Ahh, family is a beautiful thing. Poor Jonas, though. I was a horrible brother to him, I really do regret that. I think, looking back on it, maybe it was jealousy from when he was born and maybe I felt forgotten. He was the new kid on the block. I dunno. I do feel like a piece of shit for that, I'm sorry I did that, Jo, I really am. I'm also sorry that at Dad's 40th when it turned out I had an upset stomach, I went to fart on your head and shat on you instead. You were only five years old. Fuck.

But back to Coogee. The morning after the wedding we went for a swim. There were decent-sized waves, but nothing to worry about as I grew up near the beach. I was terrified but as long as I could touch the sand, stand up a little, I was fine. But about 10 minutes into my graceful dip in the water, out of nowhere I was hit with a fit. I went blind and my head started spinning. Usually I lie on the ground when I'm having a fit, not because I need to, it's just easier than trying to stand. When you are in the water you are at the mercy of mother nature. The 15-second fit seemed to last forever as I was smashed by the waves. I didn't know what was up or down and I just needed to hold my breath and pray it would stop.

It did eventually and I returned to the shore, to my family, in tears. I've never really swum with confidence since.

—

The day of the neurologist appointment came, I was called into the office, and he started by going through the MRI results . . . No lesions on the brain, so not MS . . . No brain damage . . . no nothing. My brain was perfectly fine, anatomically at least.

"Will I end up in a wheelchair?" I asked him.

In typical doctor fashion he said, "Well, not from this."

It turns out that I *didn't* have a life-ending illness. I still don't have a full diagnosis, but the doc assured me it wasn't too bad. What I have, or at least what they *think* I have, is something called paroxysmal dyskinesia, a type of episodic movement disorder a bit like epilepsy. I call it epilepsy to keep it simple for everyone.

As marvellous as not being given a death sentence was, I still faced challenges, the biggest being my fear of a fit coming on. I haven't had a fit for years and am on medication, but it doesn't take away my somewhat irrational fear, and it was this fear that led me into a deep panic-stricken anxiety spiral.

Chapter 2: **Catacombs**

EVERYTHING WENT downhill fast and that was the catalyst for what would be the next decade of my life.

Fast forward a few years and I'm travelling to Maitland, two hours north of Sydney, to do a comedy show in the middle of nowhere. I owe my career to this club and the mad old man who ran it. The gig finished late and I jumped in the car and headed home. About half way I was hit with an enormous sense of impending doom. I was hot, I felt like I was about to have a fit, everything felt wrong. So I pulled over and took a minute.

Unlike other times in my life, the panic didn't stop. Fear consumed me for the entire drive and throughout the next day. The panic consumed the next day, then another; and another and another. It felt awful. I was totally consumed, buried beneath my own uncontrollable thoughts. I was having several really bad panic attacks a day, leaving me in a constant state of fight or flight — that unconscious human response, developed over millions of years that dictates how we respond to threatening stimuli.

I'd wake up and my upper back would ache from anxiety, my neck was so stiff, and I was constantly scared. To make matters worse, I was living out of home, with three mates all on shift work who were never there and I worked a job where I looked after people with schizophrenia and I was worried I was losing my mind. No one but Clare (my then girlfriend and now wife) knew what was going on but she was at work and still lived with her parents.

—

Somehow in the middle of all of this turmoil, I had started my professional stand-up career, managed to put up new YouTube content consistently and tour the country — all while suffering more than I ever had before. Every show I did in that first year was performed in a state of panic, it was torture.

This was maybe six months into my career actually starting to flourish, a rise that I could only dream of. It was all I ever wanted and should have been celebrating every moment and every achievement but all I could think about was throwing myself off that bridge, plunging into the depths of the shipping lane below.

When this illness envelops your life, the intrusive thoughts soon come. They hit all of us at some point. Have you ever been driving along and thought, *What if I just drove into a tree?* Or when walking alongside a river, *What if I just threw my phone in the water?* Holding someone's baby, *What if I just dropped this baby?* These thoughts are horrible but they are also strangely very human. It's almost like the mind is testing you, "Hey, are you crazy? No? Good, just checking in."

Why are we so scared? And why are we so terrified of being found out for being scared? Perhaps it's that fear of being found out for who we really are that requires our lips to remain sealed and for us to defend our deepest, darkest secrets as if our lives depended on it. To wear a mask in public like we are terrified of the air we breathe. We will do anything to hide from the truth. I guess the only time we are ever truly ourselves is when we are alone in our darkest times.

So why am I on top of this shit bridge? Here, alone with the oxygen we need and the thoughts we don't?

I didn't want to die, it was the last thing I wanted, my career was going from strength to strength, my relationship was perfect, my family life was wonderful, but I couldn't stop thinking about standing on that fucking bridge and leaping off. At home, in bed, driving, at the movies, before shows, after shows, alone, in company. This intrusive fuck of a thought infected me like a virus.

You may be asking yourself, *Why in the fuck is this guy making the beginning of the book so viciously depressing, so overtly obtuse? After all, everyone has their own problems.*

Well, all I can say is, shut the fuck up, you bought my book.

But I brought this up now for two reasons. Firstly, I've never really told anyone and it's probably time I did. It's a shame really, I'm always promoting the necessity for openness between friends, family and loved ones, and yet I never told anyone. So I guess this is my coming-out party. Why didn't I tell anyone?

Clare knew I was struggling, she knew everything, but not the suicide stuff. I couldn't bring myself to tell anyone that, not even the therapist I would eventually speak to.

"Isaac, have you ever thought about harming yourself?"

"No."

Is it fear of judgement that keeps even the loudest of people so quiet? I think so. Admitting you have a problem is fucking scary and you don't necessarily have to admit it to anyone else, you can just keep quiet. But to get through it, you have to be willing to break the news to yourself. Admitting you have a problem, realising you are not infallible and understanding how human it is to be fucked up, and reaching out to someone for help is of the utmost importance.

The second reason to mention it now is because if you ever have issues in your life, real issues, disastrous ones — and I truly do believe if you haven't already, one day you will — you may need proof that there is light at the end of the tunnel and that you *can* and *will* get through it. And not just get through it, but dust yourself the fuck off and move forward, face the world with a broken smile but a smile nonetheless.

It's not easy, it's not nice or pretty and sure you may re-enter the world with some scars from your battle, but a life without scars just means you never fought your war; you ran, you hid, you never truly lived. Scars are inevitable, we are all born somewhat perfect but when we die we are broken, callused, confused, scared and alone. You can't escape it, so you may as well face it head FUCKING on.

Your body is built to scar. If you cut your skin you don't die, it heals. You scar and life goes on, and it's the same for the mind. You get wounded, you eventually heal, you scar and then move on. The scar is visible but LIFE GOES ON.

You may break, but you will heal.

You might fall, but you can get back up.

You may feel completely buried, but there is still time to take one last gasp of oxygen and dig for the surface.

Life goes on.

NB: Healing mentally takes a fuck load longer than physically. Scars are permanent memories. We find ways to accept them, maybe even disguise them, but most importantly they won't kill us.

—

I never did jump from that shit bridge and the truth is I never would have. I got help and my message to you right now is this: get help, and do not stop getting help. One day it will all be okay. I am living proof that no matter how dire things seem, there is light at the end of the tunnel. Suicide is not the answer.

This book is about a lot of things. It's a collection of ravings from a literal lunatic screaming in the figurative street, but it's also about how wonderful life is and how it can and will destroy us all if we give it the power to do so. Particularly for young men, it is a very confusing existence. We face a terribly challenging life experience and navigating it comes with vast complications, some as old as time, some very new. This book is my story of how I see the world, the madness, the ridiculous, the sad, but also the great, the powerful and the hilarious.

This isn't a self-help book — who the fuck am I to tell you what to do in your life? I'm just some dude with a beard who went to university for a few months and stopped because of the parking. Even that's a lie (see, don't trust me).

I never got into university. In Year 12 the last thing I wanted to do was study. I finished high school, drank more than I should have, worked for a year as a storeman (that's the guy who works in a warehouse and packs orders) — very fucking boring! But it was a helpful lesson. I realised then the real world sucks and it's hard to make money. Perhaps this is the reason behind this book and why I thought perhaps it could help you navigate your own challenges, determine what you do and don't need to worry about and most of all give you the written consent to go after whatever it is you truly want.

"Back to uni," said the light bulb in my head. I went for a few months to pass the course that gets you into the course you want to do, because I didn't get the marks at high school. I went to classes intermittently (because of the parking), bought the expensive textbooks I never used and somehow passed and was given the go ahead to start a degree in high school teaching.

The lesson there is don't listen to your kid's teacher, they are probably a fuckwit like me.

Oh also, for those of you playing at home, the parking bit is true. The parking at Newcastle University is fucking atrocious.

—

The point of this book, other than as an obvious money-grabbing exercise, is not just to tell some tales of my first 30 years of life but also to help guide you through yours, or the middle 30 years, or the last. Because let's face it, I'm (if I'm lucky) a third of the way through my life and this shit is running out bloody quickly.

The sands of time don't stop, you see. They don't stop for tragedy, confusion, emotion, romance or failure. They just dissipate until you look and ask, "Where did it all go?" But we will get into that shortly.

You may still be thinking to yourself, *What does this guy know?* The answer: I might be right with what I talk about here, or I might be wrong. But give me a chance. Even if you disagree with me, at least we are conversing, we are actually thinking for ourselves, we aren't just repeating what someone else has said.

This book is a tale of triumph, skill, talent and sheer beauty. I'm kidding, it's the second fucking chapter, who knows where this is going, but what I *do* know is it's designed in a way where if you have never read a book cover to cover in your life — or even if this is your 100th book — you and everyone in between will get something out of it.

I want to talk about everything we see in our lives and all we are yet to see.

If you have gotten this far and are not impressed by my erratic writing style, or maybe find me annoying, to quote the great Nelson Muntz, "Ha ha, I already have your money."

Unless you are reading this at a bookshop, then I'm fucked, but also fuck you.

Perhaps by the end, we will discover why I never decided to jump.

Shall we continue?

Chapter 3: **33.3 per cent**

> "We can easily forgive a child who is afraid
> of the dark; the real tragedy of life is
> when men are afraid of the light."
> — *Plato (or more likely Robin Sharma)*

ON THE 14th of July 2023, I turned 30. Which is horrifying. I am as old as people I used to look at and think, *Fuck, they are old.* My knees are starting to hurt, my hairline is like an elderly woman in a shopping centre carpark (accidentally in reverse) and my back is absolutely cactus.

I've often heard older people observe that they cannot believe how quickly their life has gone by and yet when we are in the thick of it we are always wishing time away. "I can't wait till I'm older." "I wish the weekend would hurry up." "Christmas holidays are only a few months away." We wish time away until all we wish for is more time.

I think 30 is pretty old in the scheme of things, particularly for 18-year-old me. If I'd looked into the future back then, I would have thought, *Married, have a house, a baby, hopefully a good job* . . . By some miracle I was right but . . .

Let's make the assumption right now that I live a healthy life, that I die of old age, happy, and content in bed with the love of my life. The average life expectancy for a man in Australia is 82.9 years, call it 83. By the time I'm that age it will increase a few more years with the help of futuristic medical interventions and science, so let's call it 90.

If I am extremely lucky, I may live to 90 years old.

As far as whether or not that is as lucky as we all think, I'm not so sure anymore. Watching family members age, I'm not overly excited about the trauma associated with getting that old, be that the falls, the frailty or the dependency on those around us. There is something about becoming a theoretical 'child' again that just doesn't excite me.

Anyway, forget that for now and say we are lucky if we get to the ripe old age of 90. This means on the 14th of July 2023 I will have completed one-third of my life — 33.3 per cent behind me, done, some of it I can't even remember anymore, and 66.6 per cent to go.

Perhaps when you first saw this book, you considered Isaac Butterfield writing a book and thought, *Why would anyone want to listen to that idiot?* (This was probably my family's reaction, if I'm honest.) You may have thought, *Is this just going to be another cheap, unnecessary autobiography?* And I understand why you would think that. It's not uncommon for a person who has some notoriety or fame to write a book, or even have a book ghostwritten (written by someone else) and expect their fans or people who like them to buy it, lap it up, and what's probably worst of all for it to have no long-lasting impact on anyone. For it to basically go in one ear and out the other. What is the point of putting pen to paper and coming out with that drivel? That's not what I want.

Sure, this is my first book, but I don't want it to be my last. I want more from this experience, and I want more for you. I want something that will affect people, help them, allow them to navigate the first third of their life and the second and the last, something to give, something to receive, a chapter to read and read again.

No, this isn't an autobiography, but this chapter is; it's a chance for you to get to know the real me, not the man you see on the screen or have heard about (positive or negative). The human that grew up, the boy who exists and the man who lives.

—

I grew up in a family with four great brothers, a famous and successful father, and a beautiful, hardworking mother. We were financially secure; not rich but comfortable. People often made that mistake about my family and me. The career my father had now attracts millions, but in the late 90s people just didn't make that kind of money.

My father, Tony Butterfield, played professional rugby league for the Newcastle Knights, and I'm so proud of everything he achieved. He came from quite a poor family and through hard work and dedication made a long-lasting career and a name for himself.

He was, and remains, my hero. I looked up to him for anything and everything. I saw him on TV, watched people ask him for his signature and even get photos with him way back when it was with an actual camera not just your phone. He won a grand final, played State of Origin and after making his debut for the Penrith Panthers in 1984, retired in Newcastle 238 games later.

Growing up with a dad who is known and loved by everyone in the town where you live is a strange way to be. At first it's great; you have amazing experiences, especially in a rugby league-mad town like Newcastle. In the late 90s and early 2000s people lived and breathed footy. With the closure of the local steel works, the town had nothing else. I was living every young boy's dream; able to go to training sessions and meet famous people; I even went on the field after the 1997 grand final (the greatest in history) and jumped on the team bus on the way home. An incredible experience which I cherish.

The notoriety of a famous father did sometimes make it hard for me though. I started playing football when I was six years old, around the same time that Dad retired from professional sport, and immediately I was compared to him. "Ohhh, you're not as good as your dad," was something I heard from my first year playing the game to when I retired 17 years later. That made it tough and, in reality, I was never really a footballer. I never had the mindset, and the toughness was never in me. The concept of running into 100 kilogram monsters didn't excite me and getting concussed for a hobby was not overly high on my "to-do list". Some people say it's a difficult sport to play if you are intelligent and I agree — I'm far too smart to bash my head into other men.

I am a good actor though, and I do respond to pressure well. I managed to pretend and play the character of a footballer's son for many years. It took me until my early twenties to actually enjoy it — up until then I just didn't have the necessary aggression.

Dad however never pushed anything on me, all he wanted was for me to do my absolute best in everything. He tried for years to motivate me, and most Christmas presents under the tree from Dad were about goal setting, motivation and doing the unbelievable. He continued this for years but as it turns out with me, and I think for many other people including him, motivation comes from within. Some people just can't be motivated by others; they have to find it in themselves.

When I told him about comedy he basically told me that's great, but that I needed to make sure I could support my family financially with whatever I did. Which is good advice. It's where people get doing something out of the box wrong. They decide they want to be X, Y or Z and then start living life like that with little to no income. It's rare that success happens for someone straight away, so if you truly want to do something that sets you apart from others, you may need to work two or three jobs to get by until you can do what you really want to. Dad taught me from a young age that I could do anything I wanted to; he is a great dad and I couldn't have been luckier.

We almost lost him twice though. He had two heart attacks a few years apart, and that really shook me. To see the person you look up to, the one who was always your hero, be floored by an invisible foe. That breaks your heart. Thankfully he is still with us.

—

My dear mum is the toughest woman I know. She met Dad while working at the Knights' head office. I have no idea what she saw in him, but here I am. They married and I came screaming into the world in 1993.

I was so lucky to get my mum, she lives for her kids and has sacrificed so much. She is a truly caring and loving individual. With my father routinely away for work throughout the years, she worked tirelessly to raise five boys. In fact, the vast majority of her past 30 years have been spent looking after my second brother, Rory. Born in 1995, he was diagnosed with autism early in his life. Today it seems every second child is diagnosed somewhere on the autism spectrum, but back then, it was rare; and even rarer was support for families in that situation.

Having a disabled child is extraordinarily difficult on relationships and families, how some couples stay together who have a child with this diagnosis I'll never know (somehow mine did). Thankfully now in Australia, we have the NDIS, which helps families with disabled kids and people with disabilities, allowing them to access support and lead a relatively regular existence.

But not back then. Rory never learnt to talk or take care of himself. This is horrible to say, but he is an adult with the mind of a three year old. It doesn't mean I don't love him or that I treat him differently, I'm just being accurate. If he had been born into a different family, or had a different mother, I really doubt he would have had anywhere near the life he has had. One of the side-effects of having a sibling with a disability is you really don't have a regular childhood; we didn't go on holidays, family outings were rare and heading out for dinner was unheard of. These, of course, are minor in the fantastic childhood I had, but you miss out on certain things. I think having a brother like Rory has made me a much better human, more patient and loving. More importantly it taught me something we all must do, and that is when you see a disabled person at the shopping centre or walking down the street you don't look the other way, don't ignore them. They know they are different, you just say hello, all they want is to be normal, regular the same as you.

———

When the third son in the family came along, five years after Rory, I, unfortunately, treated him badly. I was a shitty big brother to Jonas, which is something I really regret. I put my actions down to being jealous that he was the new kid on the block and had most of the family's attention — all the leftover attention was going to Rory. At seven years old I felt alone, but I guess that's pretty common in big families.

Darcy and Fintan turned up at some point too and

they are great blokes, I was very lucky. I have great brothers, amazing parents, wonderful grandparents, very lucky indeed. In fact it was my grandparents whom I believe shaped my mind into one that saw humour in everything. I spent almost every Friday night from age nine till 16 at their house and loved it there. My gran and pop are the best company, they were and still are two of my closest friends. Gran would swear, crack jokes and just wasn't like your regular old lady. Pop has some of the sharpest wit in the game and dad jokes are his forte. Gran would let me watch the comedies I really shouldn't have been watching and it was alongside my pop as he smoked cigarettes in the living room that I first saw Scottish comedian Billy Connolly. Without that introduction, I don't have the faintest idea of where my life would have headed.

I've lived my entire life in Newcastle, it really is god's country. From the best beaches in the world, to incredible restaurants and food, people who know Newy know it's like a small country town in a bigger city. I've been all over the world now and I can say this without a word of a lie: Newy is the best place to be.

I attended Dudley Primary School and Whitebridge High School. Here is some incredible general knowledge for you: Whitebridge High has a great hall with pictures of all the former students who have gone on to do incredible things later in life. There are a few hockey players, an Olympian or two, some footballers and, somehow, I'm not up there, so fuck them.

I was a fat kid growing up. I seemed to put weight on very easily. I just kept eating and getting bigger and bigger. I played sport on the weekends, in fact I played rugby league for 17 years and even though I trained twice a week and played once a week I still put on weight. At my biggest I was 134 kilograms (almost 300 pounds). I'm six foot eight inches so I'm big but I should never have got *that* big.

I was fat throughout school which was a green light for the bullies. In primary school, a guy called Toby punched me in the arm almost every single day for a year. Apparently I bruised easy and after he hit me he would follow it up with, "There's a bruise for tomorrow". It was strange, I hung out with the more "popular kids" (for lack of a better expression) but I was the one they all bullied.

This continued into high school, even the guy who I saw as my best friend treated me like shit. All this left me an obese teenager with no confidence, so suffice to say I was not what you'd call a "pussy magnet". I didn't kiss a girl until just before my 18th birthday. I dunno, there's just something about a tall overweight kid trying to grow a beard that just doesn't do it for teenage girls. At school, I had a few crushes but all the girls saw me as a mate, to the point where I was known in my year as "the gay friend". Now that's something to really bolster your confidence.

My relatively shitty time at school did teach me this though: a sense of humour is a must. I developed one around 10 years old as a way to make friends. In my first year of high school, I didn't know anyone, but one afternoon I made fun of a girl in class (in a nice jovial way) and by the end of it I was friends with everyone.

One of the best things that ever happened to me was being an overweight kid. As much as it absolutely sucked all the balls at the time, I wouldn't be the person I am today, with the sense of humour I have, without living through that period of my life. In saying that, if you're a fat kid without a sense of humour, you're fucked, mate.

After school I worked a lot of jobs, drank a lot (and I mean a lot of beers) and went out with my mates. There was a time there with my best mate of many years, TC, when we went out every Wednesday, Friday and Sunday night — any night we could get cheap drinks. I really enjoyed my late teenage years and early twenties, nightclubbing, a giant man standing awkwardly in the middle of dance floors, getting rejected, waking up feeling like shit. I slayed a few dragons, they will remain nameless, but holy shit there were some dragons. (I'm talking about the girls I dated if you're not following.)

I'm so glad I decided against going straight to university. I think that's one of the biggest mistakes a young person can make. You are barely in the position to wipe your own arse at that age let alone decide what career you want to do for the rest of your life (and how much debt you want to get into). I had some of the best times of my youth fucking around while many people my age spent it at uni; fuck that. In saying that, without stand-up and YouTube I'd probably be working some shitty job so why the fuck would you listen to me?

At 21 years old I met the woman I would fall in love with,

court for a while and then marry. And let's be honest, Clare needs her own chapter, so stick around for that.

—

I moved out of home at 22 and when I say "moved" my parents basically forced me out because they needed room for the rest of the family. It wasn't a great time for me but I'm glad I moved out. I changed jobs maybe 10 times during all of this, had no money, and was always waiting for tax time to come around so I could afford to do anything. I never really went on trips and I was terrified of planes — I said no to so many adventures due to that fear, a fear that now I don't even think about as I catch maybe 50 planes a year. I've also been in planes doing acrobatic tricks, barrel rolls and the like, so it's safe to say that's not a fear for me anymore. I wish I'd conquered it earlier, I didn't go to schoolies or on holidays because of it, but I have done enough dumb shit to make up for it.

I've dabbled in a little bit of drugs, a couple of joints here, a few lines of coke there (one I remember on some church steps which was interesting), but I much prefer alcohol. Nothing quite like a big day on the sauce with your mates. I have had so many great experiences doing this — also some confusing ones, like watching your mate nail his ball sack to a piece of wood and another put hot sauce in his eye (men are made differently). As I've gotten older these big "piss ups" are now few and far between, about once a year instead of every weekend.

Towards the end of the footy season, we had something

known as "Mad Monday", where we'd drink for three days straight. I'd get some sleep, while others would make it to Monday with the help of copious amounts of drugs. I'd never seen so many drugs. One Sunday morning I recall one of the boys turning up with 100 ecstasy pills — that was confronting — but every year when the stripper arrived at 5 pm on the Monday, after drinking for 72 hours you thought to yourself, *Fuck this, this is gross.*

I'm glad I grew out of it, but it was an important, and fun, experience. If you do it your whole life it's just fucking sad ... Sorry if that's a hard truth, but truth it is.

—

After about 23, when I discovered stand-up properly and was gigging regularly, my focus went from "the boys" to my relationship and my career. I can safely say I've never looked back. I lost a lot of friends and some of them I was very happy to lose; they were never great mates to begin with. I think the people who end up with the exact same group of friends in their fifties as they had in their early twenties probably never truly lived, never grew up and likely never ventured out of their comfort zone. If you can go back to your local pub or bar in 20 years' time and see the same people, doing the same things and telling the same stories, then cut them off, you don't need them.

Three years ago I bought a house, a home for my family, which was one of my best moments. As much as the shows and tours mean a lot to me, getting that place meant the world. Clare and I got married, our wedding was incredible and now we have a child, a little baby boy; well, I couldn't be any happier.

I've been on three Australian tours and a tour through the US and the UK and have performed hundreds of shows to tens of thousands of people. I've also uploaded thousands of videos and hundreds of podcasts. With a quick glance at a photograph I can be right back in any of those moments, remembering all the great times.

This isn't the end of my career, it's not even the middle, in fact this book isn't even about me, it's about you, to learn from my mistakes, consider my opinions and see what I have learnt about being a man, a relatively good man in the first 33.3 per cent of my life.

Chapter 4: **Cancelled**

How to cope and thrive with cancel culture

Since the beginning of recorded history, tribes, groups, towns and countries have identified people within their walls who do not fit the definition of a "good citizen". These people may have been violent, or dangerous, or perhaps they posed a threat of the psychological kind, like a dangerous new way of thinking. Once they were discovered, some were punished, maybe they lost a hand or something inconsequential; others were sentenced to death. If you did something really horrible, let's say you murdered someone, the sentence of death was quite just — an eye for an eye and all that reciprocal jazz. That may very well be the most final judgement and punishment available to humankind.

But it's not the worst.

There was one other punishment that really broke people. Some feared it worse than death itself exile. From Roman emperors to kings of England and even Napoleon, exile or banishment or ostracism were early versions of the cancelling we see today. It is the exact same punishment when someone is "de-platformed", be they Alex Jones, Donald Trump or even me from TikTok. The person who committed the atrocity is cast off into the universe never to be contacted, heard from, or spoken of again. They are not welcome back and they are, for all intents and purposes dead in the eyes of judge and jury, who even refuse to acknowledge they ever existed in the first place.

The difference between ancient banishment and exile, and modern cancel culture is many people nowadays don't deserve it. Sure, some do (think Bill Cosby) but some are banished from having a career, making money and being a part of society for no good reason. The worst cancellations I can think of come in two categories.

The first are those exiled for expressing an opinion: post a tweet tomorrow that doesn't fall in line with the mainstream way of thinking, I dare you. You will be attacked from all angles and people will pile on you from all sides. They will demand your workplace fires you, your wife leaves you and your kids disown you. Now some people have shitty opinions, sure, but some opinions or ways of thinking may get you banned, exiled and/or banished — all for saying things that are scientifically correct.

Tweet "Men Can't Get Pregnant"

Completely correct scientifically. Biology only works one way with that, thank fuck, and even though you are completely correct, you will be attacked. You'll be labelled a transphobe and depending on your career you may lose job opportunities, or career progression. All because you told the truth and refused to play the role the vocal minority want you to.

Tweet "The Pay Gap Isn't Real"

You are correct again, but how are you labelled? You hate women of course. You could try to explain yourself, maybe try the angle that sexism may play a role but more so it's the choices individuals make. There are more women in hairdressing than there are in engineering, more women choose to work fewer hours because they have kids, which of course is a choice, they are less likely to work dangerous jobs or move for a job. You could go on and on, but no, you hold the wrong opinion. So guess what? You are convicted of "wrong think" and you're cancelled.

Then there are jokes: jokes are dangerous. Comedy seems to be a wild west right now. You have the good, law-abiding comedians, they are on *Saturday Night Live* and headline the Melbourne International Comedy Festival Gala on the TV that no one watches, they tell safe jokes, they don't touch on race unless it's about white people, they don't dare cover gender unless it's about men. And gay jokes — no way! Straight jokes are fine though. (There is nothing wrong with joking about straight white men, just don't ban everything else, that's all I'm saying.)

Then there are the outlaws, the villains, the comedians who will joke about anything, who will cover any topic and try to find the humour in it. Think Dave Chapelle. He has produced several comedy specials in the last five years and Netflix has paid him almost $100 million. In every special, every year, people go after him, try to banish him, try to tell the people who enjoy him, *no, you shouldn't be enjoying this*! And yet he still exists.

Cancel culture goes hard after comedians because they tell jokes that are mean, that are based on race or sex or whatever taboo you can think of. So here's the question: are we all forgetting what a joke is? It's not real, dickheads! It's pretend, make-believe, much like John Wick when he kills 500 people in a movie. He doesn't get tried by public opinion for murder because we all understand he *didn't actually do it*.

The same thinking should be applied to comedy. Comedians should never shy away from jokes because they are worried about their careers being ended for doing their jobs. Comedy has been haemorrhaging authenticity ever since we started putting comedians on the TV and made them follow the TV rules, particularly in Australia. In my country this has been the status quo for a few generations, which has left many people with a skewed idea of what comedians are and what they do. Now with social media, those people are deciding which comedians are okay and which are off limits, who is allowed to be funny and even what *is* funny. On top of that, comedians themselves seem to police other comedians which is absolutely insane. The open mic comedians, the semi-pro comedians and even those at the top, if they see someone stepping outside the line they have drawn for themselves, then that person is committing thought and speech crime and must be removed from circulation as they are deemed unfit for public consumption.

The cancel squads, the Gestapo of guffaw, have never

seen real comedy. They have never really been challenged by a comedian in a dark, brick comedy venue fuelled by alcohol and an atypical thought process. They have only ever been exposed to comedians who play by the rules to get gigs and get signed by shit management companies, which is fucking boring. These comics are given gigs, they are promoted by the mainstream, but they aren't chosen by the people. They have to be, by design, far left-leaning. Perhaps they are just scared, they live their life like X (Twitter) is a first-person shooter. So when someone comes along and says something they deem offensive the shit hits the fan and they are judge, jury and executioner.

When the painfully vocal minority who run the cancel squads come for you, they want your head. They don't just want you gone, they want you dead and buried never to return. It's not just mean comments or DMs, it can actually impact your real life and your ability to work, just for a joke!

Here is a response I received after contacting a venue to hire for an event. They said no, then . . .

> "I also just want to note that Isaac Butterfield's openly homophobic, transphobic, racist, Islamophobic, misogynistic and fatphobic views do not align with —Venue Name Removed**'s own views and we would not be willing to work with him and give him a platform to continue to promote his extremely harmful ideals. All the best."

Reading that infuriates me, it's also hilarious. How could someone be so naïve? I'm a comedian, this is what I do. There is no hate whatsoever, I will never understand how someone can watch someone tell jokes on stage and become so irate. It's like going to a brothel and being upset that all the girls want is your money. Mate, if you're looking for love fuck off somewhere else.

It's not just comedians who face this furore.

Justine Sacco was an executive at a very large public company and she was jumping on a plane for a trip to South Africa. She was very excited and took to X (Twitter) to tell the world about her excitement. She tweeted, "Going to Africa. Hope I don't get AIDS. Just Kidding. I'm White."

During the 12-hour flight, the internet blew up and by the time she landed so many people were offended that her tweet went viral, she was sacked from her job, and her life was ruined. All for a joke — an offensive joke, but still just a joke.

The thing about offensive jokes and being offended by jokes is that once you've heard, that's it, you do not have to hear it again. You can avoid it, and it's not like you are wounded by it. It's not a stab wound, an illness or a broken bone, they are just words at the end of the day. To quote Australian comedian Steve Hughes, "So what? Be offended. Nothing happens!"

You are the one who has created the pain in your own mind. If this is you, look at yourself. You are so hurt by noises that others make that your reaction is to go out of your way to try to destroy their lives. This is nothing short of hilarious. Particularly when they are told *this is a joke*, something *designed* to elicit laughter. It is just beyond me that this destroys and breaks weak people so easily. Why should you be saved and protected from being offended? You're not special. All jokes are offensive to someone, literally every joke for example:

Why did the chicken cross the road? If your beloved chicken died suddenly that morning then that may offend you.

So . . .

What happened to Justine Sacco? Well, she was rehired by the company not too long after this saga, when no one cared anymore, which is the first and most important lesson in getting cancelled.

It will all be over soon.

I'm sure you are familiar with the media cycle, the concept that what is front page news today will be forgotten tomorrow. Well, strangely enough, the same concept applies to cancel culture. When someone is under attack because of a joke, or something dumb they said or did (unless they broke the law then they deserve the cancellation), their first reaction is often to panic. If they have advisors or managers they usually rush them into a forced apology, which means nothing. I'm sure we've all seen famous sports people or actors reading from a prepared script with crocodile tears as they beg to get sponsors back who dumped them because they are worried about the unnecessary and forced blowback.

I'm not sure why this is a popular reaction, surely the cancellers don't accept these apologies, I'm sure they know the jokes being told are make-believe, an act, in the same way a sexual assault in a movie isn't actually hurting anyone. But they must work, otherwise why else would this be everyone's reaction? Maybe the mob receives the apology and then drops all charges. It's like getting a call from the governor, moments before your execution, telling you that you've been saved.

Of course this isn't the case; if you apologise for a joke, you lose all credibility as a comedian. I'm not a fucking politician, I am someone who gets on stage in front of drunk people and makes them laugh. When you ask me to "*do better*" I think to myself, *Okay, I'll be more offensive next year*. The best advice I can give you, and trust me I have a lot of experience, is: *do not apologise.*

However, in saying all that, apologising is an important part of being a man. When you are wrong, when you carry on like a fuckwit, it's important to realise this and react accordingly. That is to say "I'm sorry" to the people you have hurt and vow to actually do better and be a better person from here on. As we all know, it's important to learn from our mistakes and sometimes we have to make them just to see them. But when it comes to jokes, fuck that shit. Harden the fuck up.

—

This chapter is going to take a dramatic turn, because — and you may not believe this — I am being cancelled right this very second. I'm writing this section on the 5th of February 2023 and a video I posted of a one-minute clip of jokes from a show I performed in 2022 in front of a sold-out show in Perth has gone viral. In reality, this means the internet has got a hold of it which means many of the people seeing it are not fans of offensive humour. Not enjoying offensive humour I can understand, but complaining about it, being mad about it I really don't. Just don't watch it . . .

The jokes these folk are mad at are about Aboriginal people. If you are unfamiliar with the subject, for some 80,000 years indigenous people have lived in Australia. When English settlers arrived, the white folk treated Aboriginal people horrendously. Even up until the 60s Aboriginal people were not allowed to vote, then there is the stolen generation, and massacres . . . Our history, like most histories across the world, is just horrible. In Australian comedy, if you tell jokes about Aboriginal people you are automatically a racist and this is what I have now been labelled. Which absolutely hurts me, not professionally, but personally. It really fucking hurts.

The jokes are part of a three-minute routine where I address cancel culture and discuss something I call "the cancel culture cake". I try to work out at what point or layer of the cake (each joke is a new layer) would I look at myself and think, *Fuck, that's way too far.*

I posted the video and within a few hours shit hit the fan. The number of death threats, threats against my family, threats against my dogs and my unborn son is unbelievable. But what really strikes me as unfair is the unjust misdirection the groups fuelled by anger and self-importance have. They act as if I caused the issues facing indigenous people (or insert whatever group the joke is about), when they know full well that my job is just to tell jokes.

I've been doing stand-up for almost 10 years. The jokes I tell are *not my actual thoughts*. Whether the joke is sexist or racist, homophobic or transphobic, there is no hate there. What I'm doing when I post a video like this is taking you on a journey to what it's like at a show, where anything goes, where you can talk about anything, joke about anything, because everyone there agrees to enter a "comedy contract". They know offensive jokes may be told but they are told just to offend people and believe it or not, to offend myself. The jokes I included in that video, when I first wrote them, offended me — that's why I wrote them. I wanted to include the worst of the worst as a part of the recipe of the cancel culture cake.

The misdirection I speak of is really strange. Activists and regular angry people who just stumble across something they don't like will spend hours, days or weeks arguing about what a piece of shit I am rather than actually helping the community they are fighting for! This is nothing but a hoax. They feel like they have achieved something but in reality, my career is fine because I'm a comedian and comedians tell jokes. Meanwhile, the community they so desperately want to help remains in the same position they left them in. They believe they have won but in reality everything just stays the same.

If I said right now I wasn't nervous I'd be lying. I am watching my back when out in public and this is normal for most people in my position. This kind of heat does die down quickly but for the first few days leaving the house can be worrying, all it takes is for one dickhead to think they are a hero and take you on. My bigger fear is what if someone bumps into Clare and hurts her or the bub? For the next week or so we will probably lay low.

But I'm also angry. People who know me, know that I am the furthest thing from racist. I'm pro changing the date of Australia Day to help unify indigenous and non-indigenous people. I want more funding for young kids in central Australia

— they should have as much access to education, hospitals and resources as anyone else. I think we should learn about our indigenous history and realise we are probably closer than some ancestor who came here 200 years ago from Scotland. And it makes me angry because people then react like none of my real opinions exist and the jokes I make (and we are all guilty of fucked-up jokes, not just comedians) are my real thoughts on living human beings. That is absolutely insane.

I don't hate anyone but I will attack everyone if it makes people laugh and I won't back down from that.

What has helped me get through this is the fact that this is my fourth time being cancelled. Maybe "cancelled" isn't the word, people attempt to cancel you, and some have said to me over the past few days, "No one is trying to cancel you" which is somewhat hard to believe because #cancelisaacbutterfield was trending. But I am probably prepared for this better than most. Let me tell you the tale of how I became probably the most hated person (at least to easily offended people) the first, the second and the third time.

The third time wasn't too interesting — actually maybe the Aboriginal joke was the fifth time — but anyway, I was booked to go on Dr Phil's TV show after I made a video about women's body hair, but due to COVID it never eventuated. That may have been the third and a half time I was cancelled. The actual third time was when I made a joke about a jumping castle tragedy that happened in Tasmania. An awful event that broke the community. The joke was dark, it was fucked up, that was the point. There were a few news articles and the premier of Tasmania wanted me banned but that was about it.

As for the first and second cancellations, well, they were unbelievable experiences . . .

In 2019 I booked two weeks of shows at the Melbourne Comedy Festival. It was the first time I performed a whole new 60-minute show. It was daunting, it was scary, and on opening night I had a notepad on stage with the jokes on it. By the end of that two weeks I had a tried-and-tested hour that would go on to become my first special and was performed in 90 shows to people all over the world.

The joke was about a vegan person being at my show, and that particular vegan saying something along the lines of, "Hey, if you get to know me, maybe you'll change your views on vegans forever." I follow that up with, "That's like a Jew in 1942 turning up at Auschwitz and saying, 'Hey, maybe you should get to know me'." The crowd would laugh and then I'd follow that up with (talking about the vegan) "So we gassed the cunt."

Now when comedy is written on a page out of context, it's pretty shit and loses almost all its punch, but this got great responses all over the world, even in front of many Jewish audience members — except for one and she sent me an email. It was an extremely angry email, where she said something along the lines of, "I enjoyed your show, I laughed at everything." (So everything was funny except when it was about her, funny that.) "But how dare you say that about Jewish people, you should never joke about the Holocaust."

It's a common denominator among the cancelling army to think it's funny until it's about them. Unfortunately when I received this email I was just about to walk on stage. I was behind the curtain with my music starting to play as I read this, so I was firing on all cylinders, I was pumped ready to go and I replied with, "If you can't stand the heat get out of the oven!" A hilarious comeback to a heckle may I say, but I regret it somewhat.

The lady who sent me the email wasn't in the audience. And she wasn't expecting a humorous comeback, and it *was* humorous. She was sitting at home and copped a pretty brutal rebuttal. She probably copped it home alone and even though she was being pretty mean to me, maybe I should have saved it just for a good story and punchline on stage.

A few days later I received an email from the crime reporter at the *Herald Sun* in Melbourne.

"I have been contacted by the Anti-Defamation Commission about a complaint following your gig at the Australian Institute of Music in Melbourne on April 11.

"The complainant says you made an offensive comment to the effect of 'imagine the joy of people when they heard the Jews were sent to the gas chambers'.

"I have received a copy of the complaint she made and your response which reads 'If you can't stand the heat, get out of the oven.'

"I am intending to write a story about this. Can I please get a response by 3 pm today?

"The ADC has called on you to formally apologise for these comments. What is your response?

"I note there is a petition circulating for you to run for federal parliament. Is this a genuine ambition?"

Reading that the *Herald Sun*, a big newspaper, is going to do a story on you is pretty daunting. I did panic quite a bit, but I absolutely did not reply; this is comedy after all. I'm not going to apologise and if you want to hear my reasoning then don't read the *Herald Sun*, come over to my YouTube channel and hear it from the piece of shit's mouth, AKA me.

This was just the start of the cancellation process; it was quickly nationwide then worldwide. Absolute madness. From America to England, even *The Times of Israel* came out and reported on me. "Netflix drops Aussie comic over gas chamber joke." (Quick side note, we never had a deal with Netflix. That was all part of marketing my special; all I said is we were in talks with a big streamer and they dropped it, but the media ran with it and claimed it was Netflix.)

Then came the death threats and the angry emails. It quickly subsided as it always does, but it helped sell out the rest of my tour and that's what most people don't understand about cancellations: it's actually great for business. As long as you don't mean what you're saying and you are just doing it to make people laugh then you will be perfectly fine.

Then, a few weeks go by and it's like nothing ever happened. Everything returns to normal and calm settles on the cancellation front.

And for 18 months there were no other cancellations to speak of, a few minor controversies but nothing dramatic. I had written and performed new shows across the world, filmed a live special at the Enmore theatre in Sydney in front of 2000 people and released it on Amazon Prime (this one was actually rejected from Netflix due to it being "too

Australian". Apparently it wouldn't translate to a worldwide market).

Then one afternoon, six months or so after the special was released, I had all but forgotten about it. I was working on a new hour of comedy, and in the mists of COVID, *boom*, the shit hit the fan again and I was front-page news once more. A Muslim man of high regard in that community clipped a bit from my show about the Christchurch Massacre and reposted it on Twitter. It was an awful event, where 51 people were murdered in cold blood, an event that ruined and changed lives all around the world and I joked about it on stage.

The bit goes like this:

"The saddest thing about the Christchurch massacre wasn't the innocent Muslims who died, it was the hundreds of people who couldn't get home from nightclubs that night in Christchurch because all the cabbies were dead."

A poor taste joke, but a joke nonetheless and fuck me sideways the shit hit the fan. I had 60,000+ death threats and abusive messages in the first 48 hours. I had never seen so much anger; everyone wanted my head.

But this is comedy, ladies and gentlemen, that joke is a dark, dark joke but still, a joke. Am I happy Muslim people died? Of course not. That would be horrific. I should be fucking put down if I thought like that. No, I just said the most inappropriate turn of phrase at that very moment. I had performed that show, as I said, all over the world, from

Sydney to London, Edinburgh to Christchurch itself, and everywhere I would get an applause break after that joke, even in Christchurch. The audience loved how horrible it was and my audience included Muslim people who also liked it.

The one thing I really noticed while in the thick of being cancelled, is that people tell you you're not funny or that joke wasn't funny, even though they just watched a theatre of people laugh at that exact joke. Sure, comedy is subjective, but it seems that in this strange religious-like mindset the (and I don't like using this term) "woke" live in — and this includes activists, feminists and anyone who changes their Instagram bio to support whatever movement is trending at that moment — they demand you listen to them because they are the deciding factor in humour. Have they never had a conversation in a bar or pub? Fucking harden up.

They will not countenance that things can be just a joke. They take everything far too seriously and believe words are violent. I was told after the Aboriginal bit went viral that I was responsible for the suicides of Aboriginal teenagers. Of course I wasn't, but people genuinely believed that someone telling a joke on stage was this harmful.

Their religion is outrage, they dedicate their lives to it, they wake up every morning looking to be offended, they follow people on Twitter they know will upset them, it gives them a sense of belonging, almost a higher power to believe in, they subscribe to all the ideologies and if you don't, you better believe the other devotees will come for you and you better fall into line or you will become a pariah.

One way people will try to get to you, to really hurt you, is through the gaps in your armour. Everything has been said to me, and about me, hundreds of times. Every kind of insult and death threat you can imagine. People have spread lies, they have made videos, podcasts, TikToks, everything, so I have pretty thick skin, like your grandfather's heel, tough as an old boot. But when people want blood they will get it by any means necessary and when you have people messaging your wife in droves telling her that they hope she miscarries, that is hurtful, I won't lie. She took it all in her stride. Clare was bullied mercilessly in school and she looked at these weak pieces of shit like they were nothing. She ignored them and laughed at them more often than not. I'm very proud of her for that. Being the first lady of a professional arsehole isn't an easy gig.

They will go after friends and some people — whom I know very well and have had over for dinner at my house — bowed to the pressure and unfollowed me. One young lady from a semi-successful TV show in Australia came to the show, saw the jokes live, loved it and even bought the merch. But then people started complaining, sending her messages, angry at her for following me, because if she follows me she must agree with everything I have ever said. So she cut me off.

People get very weak and very scared when the barbarians are at the gates, but we must show resolve, particularly when we haven't done anything wrong. The moment we show weakness and let the angry mob win, they feel powerful, they think they are in command and they start to enforce their rules on others. They see themselves as the almighty and feel drunk with power. This can all be avoided however. Here's the comedian's three-step guide in the event that you get cancelled.

1. If you actually did something horrible, well, you're

fucked.

Killed someone, hurt someone, sorry fuckface, you deserve it.

2. Don't apologise.

Stand by what you did, especially if it was a joke. We should all stand by our jokes because they are jokes and not real (it feels ridiculous having to write that but some people really have to hear it). Every time I was cancelled I didn't comment to the media or to anyone else. I made videos on my YouTube channel and discussed everything there. I did this in the hope the logical-minded in the mob might take a moment and see that this guy isn't the boogey man we think he is. The only time I was ever truly upset with peoples' reaction to these videos was after the Aboriginal bit and people were messaging me saying they hated my apology and my apology should have been better. It wasn't an apology, dickhead, what are you talking about?

3. Wait.

The crazy thing about cancellations is they never last; cancelling people isn't real. You only get cancelled if you cancel yourself. Cancel culture *is* real, there is an actual cultural movement to cancel people we don't like, but *you* can't be cancelled. Anyone who is anyone in the comedy game has been cancelled and 99.9 per cent of them are doing fine; Joe Rogan, Jimmy Carr, Louis CK — they are all fine. The only comedian who is actually cancelled is Bill Cosby, I wonder why that is . . . oh yeah, he did something truly horrible. He didn't just slightly offend some thin-skinned individuals who express every feeling they have on Twitter.

And that's it, that's all it is.

—

Unfortunately, cancellation isn't just reserved for people in my profession, it's a threat to everyone. Maybe you have an old tweet where you made a particularly gay slur, or you dropped the N-bomb when you were 12. Maybe you winked at Sharon in the office, or said hello to Kim in accounts with too much gusto. We can all be cancelled for anything at any time, all it takes is for someone to make enough of an emotional plea and *boom*, it's viral on social media and before people go to sleep at night they want to make you hang yourself with a noose. It's a weird and wild world out there, ladies and gents, but with my three-step approach I think we will all be just fine.

The thing is, cancellations aren't just reserved for jokes. JK Rowling has been cancelled. She received death threats and rape threats and has been the target of all manner of outrageous discourse, just for sharing her opinion. Unfortunately for JK, her thought process does not align with the recommended beliefs we all must have. As a woman she believed that the most extreme trans lobby beliefs affected women in an unfortunate manner.

From my understanding, most trans people just want to live normal lives, but some others have more extreme ideas; they want to dissolve the concept of a man and a woman altogether. JK had some things to say about that, the most well-known in response to an article published during the pandemic giving menstrual hygiene advice to "people who menstruate". JK responded with, "I'm sure there used to be a word for those people. Someone help me out. Wumben? Wimpund? Woomud?" She then continued with "A Vile Rant" about the fact sex (biological) exists!

The reaction? All-out war on her and every single thing she has ever created. Harry Potter was cancelled, Fantastic Beasts was cancelled, Hogwarts Legacy was cancelled. She was labelled a transphobe, a TERF (trans exclusionary radical feminist) and they demanded she apologise.

She didn't.

In fact, she doubled down. This meant she wasn't invited to events, a Canadian artist removed her name from the books she wrote, the actors from the films of her books wrote an open letter to any idiot with enough time to read them disavowing her — which I'm sure they did because they themselves were under duress by the angry mob.

JK Rowling, under the pressure of death threats, a fatwa on her head, stuck to her beliefs. That is bravery. They came for her but she refused to yield. She believes she is correct and logical scientifically minded people tend to agree with her "violent statements".

Her trauma from this is a lesson for all of us. You must speak the truth as you see it, do your research and be focused when you deliver it, understand they will come for you, but hold your ground. You will see others around you crumble due to their own feeble constitution, but you must hold fast. Hold fast long enough and you will rise from the ashes of battle with your integrity intact and your ideas holding true.

Chapter 5: **Decisively engaged**

I REMEMBER saying to Clare in 2016 or so, "This is our only option, we have no other choice, either this works or we fail." By this stage, I had a few years of stand-up comedy under my belt, but I knew the only way to really succeed was to embrace the "new" and go all in on YouTube. Back then, most regular comedians looked down on internet comedians. Not me. I knew it was the perfect way to reach an audience. Why spend years performing to tiny crowds in the back of a bar with the hope that a TV or radio producer will "discover" you when you could be making videos and performing weekly to *millions*?

The people I started out with in the comedy game immediately hated me. Not just the open mic comedians, I'm talking about the "pros" at the Melbourne Comedy Festival, the people who write safe jokes and suck the right dicks. They saw YouTube as a "hack" thing to do, but I didn't give a fuck. I knew my way was the right way. YouTube and building an audience was the goal.

At the time, I was working in a job that was standard income for someone with little to no qualifications and Clare was working in retail and really suffering. I hated seeing her deal with the shit that retail workers have to deal with, she had to deal with some of the worst humans on earth, both customers and colleagues. We made enough, but we were both still living with our parents and could afford to go out once a week, but we knew that we wouldn't achieve the life that we wanted if we continued to just coast along.

My job was good, I worked in marketing and video production and didn't mind it one bit, I actually liked it. I worked hard for a few hours a day and got to go home in the early afternoon. All I had to say was, "I've got a meeting" (much to the receptionist Irene's dismay) and I was out of there. I thought I could do this job for a while, but I was never going to own a home on this wage, never going to be able to set my children up, or take them around the world. More importantly, if I stayed where I was, I'd never forgive myself for not doing what I *really* wanted to do. I'd die with a heart full of regret. I needed stand-up. I needed to be a comedian. I knew I could be successful, I just had to work out how.

But the far more pressing issue was Clare. She was working for a large department store at the time and was getting mercilessly bullied. I needed to get her out. Clare was young and they wanted to bring her down a peg or two, teach her that there was nothing to smile about, that you should hate your partner and that you are a victim in life and there is fuck all you can do about it but grow old and sour. I had to give us a chance at a life where we could live with freedom, happiness and avoid the plight of the downtrodden.

My daily work schedule looked a little something like this: 6 am: I'd arrive at work before the boss so I could leave early and people wouldn't ask questions

6.30 am: Coffee
7 am: Coffee and watch YouTube
7.15 am: Shit
7.15–11 am: "Work"
11–11.30 am: Morning tea
11.30 am–1 pm: "Work" then skip lunch so I could leave early
1 pm: Go to a "meeting"/home so I could work on YouTube videos

Once I was home I could do what I really wanted to do, and that was write. Writing had become second nature to me. I would just sit down and the ideas would flow. It's a very strange process to see at one moment an empty page and have no idea what you will write about, then moments later a story starts to form and almost like you have downloaded something from the ether, there it is, you birth something onto a page. Regrettably, what I was writing was mostly sex jokes and bullying vegans — not exactly changing the world — but if you ignore the content I'm basically Shakespeare.

Making videos on the other hand was new to me. A very strange concept in the beginning and I struggled to write, perform, edit and publish a video to go out into the world each week. To be judged and hopefully grow my channel was daunting. But I learnt fast and being in charge of what I really wanted to do was such a liberating feeling. I've been uploading videos on two different channels without fail for four years now.

Unfortunately my work ethic was never the best, I was nothing like the great cricketer Donald Bradman who would practise out the back of his house hitting a golf ball with a cricket stump into a panel of corrugated iron to get his eye perfect. I wasn't Mozart, either, practising and composing nine hours a day. I was lazy, very lazy, and sure I wrote, but not enough. I worked somewhat hard, but nowhere near enough, which is a wonderful lesson — regardless of how hard you feel like you are working and no matter what your achievements are in hindsight you'll realise you weren't working anywhere near full capacity.

I guess I lacked confidence. I kept putting off making the videos, which is something I've done with so many things throughout my life. Its always easier to avoid starting something new or difficult, but this one night, after I wouldn't stop talking about how I really needed to start making YouTube videos, Clare said to me, "Just do it. What are you waiting for? If you fail then so be it, but just try."

I thought, *Fuck it, she's right. So what if people laugh at me? Or my friends pick on me? Let's give it a crack.* The next day I bought a brand-new $2000 camera and audio set-up from a local camera shop. And then . . . nothing. I did nothing. I'd taken the first step, but then I hesitated.

That shit sets you back. And it's even harder to get going the second time. You've lost momentum, you shame yourself for stopping, and this time it's harder because you have the added guilt of a $2000 camera you can't afford.[1] You can't help thinking, *I should have just gone balls to the wall and fucking started!*

Luckily I was able to use that camera in my day job. The bosses, who I really did like, encouraged me to think outside the box when it came to marketing. The company was a huge multi-national freight company, we delivered parcels to people's doors, so how the fuck do you market that shit? It's harder than it looks, no one wants to follow a parcel delivery service on social media. The only time they have anything to do with their social media was to complain about a missing parcel or some dickhead driver doing something stupid.

My plan was to gain the public's trust in my hometown by providing them with something of value. So I started making videos about the town's history, places to eat, things to do, even the haunted places; all to gain the public's trust. It taught me a very important lesson: aiming small to grow. But that's a chapter in itself.

The great thing about the meaningless videos I was making was that I had to teach myself how to film, write, produce and edit. I was a one-man band. If you want to be a

---

[1] You don't need to buy a $2000 camera like me. What are you, fucking stupid? You need an iPhone and decentish audio and then you are sweet.

content creator this is paramount. You really can do it yourself and you can learn it all on YouTube. If you think you can't, that's just another excuse. Everything is there: how to turn the camera on, how to shoot with it, how to adjust the ISO; what the fuck is an ISO? I didn't have an editor helping me out until I had been on YouTube for four years.

The internet is this amazing free resource where you can learn basically anything from surgery to how to buy crypto. The generations before us used the excuses "Oh I don't know how to do it" or "I don't understand it". But that isn't true anymore. If you have a connection to the internet you have an infinite source of knowledge. You don't need university, you don't need college — don't get me wrong, if you wanna be a doctor you need to go to uni — but not for anything else. Teach yourself how to do things, don't rely on others, and put yourself in the best possible position so when your time comes you are so fucking ready you are almost jumping out of your skin.

—

Time went by and I got fired from that multi-national freight company (can't imagine why). I picked up work here and there but still I wanted comedy to be my life. At this point it was basically the sport I played on the weekend. It was my passion and my hobby but I wanted to make money from it.

Then Clare hit me with it again. I'd just returned home after opening for fellow Australian comedian, Frenchy.

Frenchy is an Australian comedian whom I love and a great mate of mine. He and another guy by the name of Josh Wade, who I'm still friends with and who also managed my early career, were people whom I went on the road with and opened for. I loved it. I got a taste of what real touring was like, what fame was like. I experienced having a crowd lose their shit and being so pumped when they stand and cheer for you. I have some amazing memories of those trips, but when I'd get home, going to work the next day was fucked. I knew comedy was what I wanted to be doing, so I wasn't trying to find better jobs, but also I wasn't doing anything about kicking my career up the arse.

One evening Clare told me again, "If you don't do it, you'll regret it." Thank god for her. It also happened to be the very same evening that West Indies cricketer Chris Gayle was really creepy with a female journalist on TV. She asked how he felt his innings was going and he replied, "I want to come and have an interview with you, that's why I'm here. Just to see your eyes for the first time. Don't blush, baby." The reporter continued the interview, but was obviously shaken by him being a big old creeper. No surprises but the video of the interview went viral.

I thought to myself, *Okay, here is a chance to make something, let's see how it goes?*

So I made a shitty little video of my own, maybe 90 seconds long, impersonating the cricketer and the journalist. I grew some balls, edited it and posted it. And guess what? It did well on Facebook. Maybe 50,000 views in a few hours. Fuck me, I was blown away. People were tagging friends and

I was getting laughing emojis. Clare saw the look my eye and said, "This is it, this is what you need to do!"

I sat with that knowledge in my head for a few days, and then something clicked. I've never been able to describe exactly what it was until recently when I read Jocko Willink's book *Extreme Ownership*. Jocko is a former US Navy Seal and one of the most mentally tough people on the planet. In his book, he uses the phrase "decisively engaged". It's a military term meaning you must win *because there is no retreat.*

That's what had clicked when I made and posted that video, I was *decisively engaged.*

A few nights later I sat down and told Clare, "I'm going to do it. I'm going to go all in because it *has* to work. There is no other option." That's word for word what I told her. "It *has* to work."

We had no other choice. I wanted to be successful and challenge myself to achieve something I'd always wanted — to be a comic — but more importantly I wanted a stable future for the ones I love and I was sure this was the way to get there. I gave myself no excuses, no fallbacks and no options. The only way was forward. I vowed to Clare that I would achieve this; I didn't quite know how, but I told her that I would do it and would refuse to accept anything less.

If you are decisively engaged, if you give yourself no other option, if you do whatever it takes to win, then you will get there in the end. It takes work, practise, sacrifice and dedication, and if you don't allow yourself to lose then winning is the only option. This relates to anything — learning another language, getting a degree, getting fit, whatever. If you are *decisively engaged* then who the fuck will take that away from you? No one!

Even though I'd made a decision that would ultimately change my life — and had tested the water with the Chris Gayle video — I still lacked self-confidence and self-belief. I didn't know if people would find my stuff funny or entertaining and the mates I surrounded myself with weren't helping. My friends in my late teens and early twenties were all blokes I played football with and the vast majority were shit people who hated anyone who stuck their head above the crowd— the sort who try desperately to bring others down to their level of weakness. Like someone drowning next to you, they will do everything in their power to pull you down to help them get one more gasp of oxygen. They tried that with me when I started doing open mic nights, they said shit like, "What are you doing that for?" and "You're *not* funny!". They hated anything new. They hated it if you broke away from the pack mentality and that's why most of them will probably die with the same mindset they had when they were 20.

These people lowered my confidence to such a low level that I was overcome with so much self-doubt I feared the rest of the world would feel the same way about me that my mates did. I thought to myself, *If I'm going down, I'm taking someone with me.* So I got some help from two old friends who'd always had my back, Josh Bluey Nelson and Morgan Brown. Josh, who you may know from the *Cancel Me Now* podcast, was there from the very beginning. And Morgan was great too, filming countless early videos. The three of us sat down at Bluey's house one morning and discussed our first video, *A Dickhead's Guide to Newcastle*; basically jokes about our hometown that only locals would understand.

Having those two around me changed my mindset. We were all vulnerable but we trusted the jokes and we knew it would work. As with anything, the first time is scary and when we posted our first video to Facebook and YouTube, we were absolutely shit scared. But we watched the numbers go up and up and up . . . 100 shares . . . 1000 shares . . . 200,000 views! It was incredible. It was so good we were on the radio the next day talking about it.

From that point I had the bug. This was *exactly* what I needed to be doing. We made a second video, and then other ones about sporting events and other stuff in the news. But we were still working our 9 to 5 jobs and finding it hard to carve out the time to meet, write and film. In the end, Bluey and Morgan had to get back to their other lives, but because I'd removed the option of retreat, I said, "No, I will *not* give up." I could have easily lost motivation and momentum but because I was decisively engaged, I didn't.

I fucking doubled down.

I continued making videos on my own, which again was terrifying, but now I had a bit more confidence. I made two every single week for a year before one went viral. If you're an idiot and are unaware of how many weeks there are in a year, there are 52, so that's over 100 videos — or a 1 per cent strike rate.

Up until this point I had never been a hard worker, not in school, not in sports, work, anything. I always looked for the path of least resistance. Taking this approach will get you a calm sea to travel — your life will be safe — but rarely will it be worthwhile. So how the fuck did I go from someone who avoided work at all costs to someone who craved being busy? Was it drive? Passion? Self-belief?

Nope, it was mental illness.

Around the time I started making videos with Bluey and Morgan I moved out of home. Which is a confronting time for any young person but I also started experiencing severe panic attacks again. It was a tough time. I felt very lost. I started missing shifts at work because I didn't feel comfortable driving. I didn't feel comfortable at home or anywhere else either. I was experiencing anxiety pretty much from the moment I woke to the moment I went to sleep. The only time I didn't feel this tidal wave of fear was when I buried my head in the laptop. Whenever my brain was busy, it wasn't malfunctioning. It wasn't overactive. It was finally calm and I loved it.

So I worked in every spare moment. Whenever Clare was at work and I wasn't, I worked. Whenever I had a break or an early mark from my day job or whenever I took a day off, I worked. Having that place to bury my head and write was a massive relief.

Thankfully, my brain is 95 per cent recovered from that tumultuous period, but I still reap the benefits of what I learnt from that time. I still bury my head and write every day and that's how I'm able to make videos for several channels, do podcasts, write stand-up material and a book. I love work. I have rewired my brain and developed the habit of extreme productivity. The benefit of that stressful time? I finally have something I genuinely enjoy and I'm so fucking happy all of this came from one decision: I made the choice to be decisively engaged.

—

It all could have easily gone the other way. How many people have you heard say, "I wish I did this" or "I wish I followed that dream"? For many people, if not most people, regret and wasted opportunity is their homeostatic state. It's what defines them. Fuck that. You have the power to change shit in your life, you really do, it's just most of us choose not to. Either you're too busy, or too stressed, or whatever. It's all bullshit. Sure some of us start from better positions than others but, plain and simply, that's life. You have the exact same 24 hours in a day as anyone else and if you are privileged enough to have a phone and internet connection then guess what, fuckface? You can get to wherever you want, as long as you work hard, spend the time and do the reps. Then, when you are called up, you are so fucking prepared, you stroll in like a gangster.

I maintain this attitude to this day. Why? Because I *can't* fail. I *can't* fall behind. I won't let what I've already done define how I see myself. People in the comedy game ask me all the time, "How do you make so much content?" Well, this is my job. It's not a fucking hobby, not a side project or a hustle. Every day I get up like I'm going to work and I get done what I need to get done.

I have three priorities:

Family is number one. That's why every night at 6 pm, I switch off and spend the evening with Clare, Atti and the dogs.

Second priority is work. Everything has to be done, be that videos filmed, emails sent, partnerships organised, whatever. I can't switch off unless that's happened.

And third priority is health. I have to train but really I add that to my workday. I consider it work. I have to be at the gym every day or I'm not getting everything done that has to be done. That routine is what allows me to hit the goals I set for myself each and every week.

Keeping a routine is everything when it comes to trying to chase something out of reach. Every great, successful person has these things in common: passion, drive, routine and no other option. These days, my routine is as follows:

6 am: Wake up and play with Atti
6.05 am: Coffee
8 am–12 pm: Work
12–12.30 pm: Walk the dogs
12.30–2 pm: Work
2–5 pm: Gym, groceries and whatever else needs to be done
6 pm: Clock off time, family time

Some people say jumping into work as soon as you wake up is not ideal, but I disagree. That huge spike of cortisol in the morning fires me up to work flat out for a few hours. After that, a leisurely stroll with the dogs brings me gently back to reality.

This routine works perfectly for me. Touring is different, and my routine changes if I'm on the road or have meetings or podcasts with people overseas but, by and large, it's the same every day. I create the same amount of content when I'm on the road. You may have noticed when other comedians on YouTube go on tour their content stops. Not mine. I know there are people all over the globe who depend on me putting out videos to take them away from their lives; a small distraction to hopefully put a smile on their face. I will not let them down.

I only write stand-up material at night, with a whiskey in hand, and while listening to Mozart. Yep, I write dick jokes to Mozart. I always have. I started doing it a long time ago and I think I always will. The lack of lyrics helps me lose myself in the music. It somehow blocks the world out and allows me to find that creative flow state.

I've seen way too many people treat comedy as a hobby, and that's why the average internet comedian's career is only two years. Two years? That's nothing. That's so short that it makes professional sport look like a life-long career. If I live for 80 years and have to work for 60 of those, I would have 58 years filled with something other than comedy and thinking about what could have been. That terrifies me and I won't let that happen.

Those who treat comedy as a hobby will go the way of anyone who treats something they really want with disrespect. They may say they really want this relationship to work but they aren't putting in the effort and it will fail. They may say they want to lose weight but they are stuffing their face and haven't been to the gym in a week. It's this disrespect to ourselves, and the people we dream of becoming, that ultimately sees us in a nursing home full of regret.

By being decisively engaged, by not giving yourself another option, by refusing to surrender, by taking no backwards steps, *that* is the best way I know to achieve success, however you define it. At the very least, it's the beginning of earning it. You are on your way. You're moving forward because you're on the precipice of greatness. You can't go backwards. Why would you want to?

Chapter 6: So you're going to be a dad

I HAD no idea what to feel. Nothing had changed and yet *everything* had changed.

Clare and I decided we wanted to be parents early on in our relationship. We were pretty happy with everything in our lives but we needed something more — we wanted a little one. One little version of ourselves. We decided that we would come off birth control several months before our wedding and then start trying closer to the big day — but not too close as to ruin the honeymoon with morning sickness.

To cut a long pornographic story short, I impregnated Clare extremely quickly — I am the eighth wonder of the natural world! Somebody fucking stop me! I won't go into the gory details of how that transpired as my family or my baby may read this one day, but let's just say Clare is a trooper, and what a god awful experience it must have been for her.

But I had fun . . .

One night a little while later, I was lying in bed, ready to go to sleep and Clare yelled out, "OMG, come here!" And there it was — a pregnancy test showing the faintest line, so faint to the point you don't quite believe your eyes. She tested, tested and tested again — quite literally 20 tests over a week — before we decided to head to the doctor for a professional opinion. That moment waiting for those lines to appear can instil blinding fear and absolute joy at the same time. It's a feeling of moving fast and standing still all in the same moment. I'm sure it can illicit other emotions if you don't know the person very well and definitely weren't trying.

For me, the fear came in waves. Firstly from a purely selfish point of view: my life was about to change forever and I might not be able to do the little things that made me happy. Could I still go to the gym? Could I still catch up with a mate? Could Clare and I still go to dinner or a movie . . . *Everything* was going to change and, honestly, I'm a man of routine. I *hate* change.

What you're feeling, in reality, is not selfishness, but *anxiety*. You're scared. You're not a bad person! You're just a child who isn't aware of how old you are. I'm sure you've felt this way at various points throughout your life — maybe before you started or left a job, or started or ended a relationship. And what do most of us do when we feel this way? We self-sabotage or, at the very least, we have sabotage-like thoughts. It's natural to not want things to change. Why change when things are comfortable? Every single thing I have ever done in my life that has either been successful or a learning experience was borne out of fear, anxiety and defeating that inner self-sabotaging bitch, desperate to hide under the blankets.

Thankfully, the fear of a baby quickly dissipated.

As I write this chapter, Clare is 14 and a half weeks pregnant and I'm sitting next to her while she sleeps on a plane flying from Perth to Sydney. We have just done two shows over two nights with over 1000 people at each. Clare, as usual, has been amazing, selling merch like a demon. She's been sick and tired, her body is changing, and it's so difficult for her to keep up with it. I am genuinely in awe of what she's capable of. I also now know we're having a son and we have decided to call him Atticus, which means "man of Attica". Attica is the ancient area that surrounds the Greek city of Athens. It's a masculine name, a strong name, one of power, but also of delicate intellect, dating back thousands of years. I guess it's just a name, but the way I see it, it gives him a fighting chance in this ever-changing and confusing existence we find ourselves in.

Names are so important. It's the first impression you make, the first word out of your mouth when you introduce yourself. It's the key to unlocking the folder of memories tucked away inside the hippocampus. Saying someone's name inside your mind right now unlocks a myriad of past memories, thoughts and feelings. That's all in a name. So we took great care in naming him Atticus. First of all, obviously, we had to do the school test — what rhymed with this boy's name? *Smatticus* . . . *Splaticcus* . . . I guess *Fatticus*, but really there is nothing and that's the first test. Shout out to the dipshit parents who named their kid Lucas which of course on day one of school will be called Lucas Spewcas, Ella Don't Smell Her, Celeste Molest and if you have watched enough *Seinfeld* you can forget Dolores.

I never got called many names. Bullies found other ways. Although I did have a teacher in Year 3 who decided at school assembly to call me Isaac Margarine Meadow, so that was on him. The tables have turned . . . He's now dead.

As soon as we named our son Atticus, I felt immediately bonded to him. No longer did I see him as a baby in the womb. He was real, my son, the human I am responsible for, the reason I work, write, perform, make videos and wake up — or at least that's one of the reasons. There is also his mother, of course, without whom none of this would be possible.

Becoming a parent is terrifying and chances are if you aren't terrified, you aren't going to be a very good parent. You *should* be scared, you will be in charge for their formative years. The littlest of things can break a young person.

Recently I was reading the Hungarian–Canadian physician Gabor Maté. He writes a lot about the first three years of a child's life, on interactions between parent and child; tiny things like picking them up when they cry. When you teach your kid that they are welcome and that they are loved, their personality becomes more trusting. They react to things based on love and caring, not fear and anger. This is especially important when it comes to their fathers. So be with your fucking kids, gents! Bring them into this world and give them the best possible chance. Do everything that your parents didn't, and succeed where they failed. Pick them up, love them or face the consequences, because, as Gabor says, "Trauma is a psychic wound that hardens you psychologically ... that then interferes with your ability to grow and develop. Trauma is not what happens to you, it's what happens inside you as a result of what happened to you." Every single thing that's wrong with us as adults is borne out of trauma. With your kid you have a clean slate, so keep it sacred.

You're probably thinking that's easy for me to say; I'm a new father. But you better fucking believe I will do without sleep. I will shoulder the stress. Whatever the fuck I need to do to give him the best chance at growing up without fear and seeing the world as the beautiful place it can be, I will do it.

In saying all of that I'm still scared.

I'm no longer afraid of having a child, but I'm shit scared of the idea that they are completely dependent on me to provide for them both physically and emotionally. How do I keep this little creature alive, safe and protected? I am quietly confident Clare and I will be great parents and do this with ease, but what about financially? I need to make sure I do everything in my power to provide for both Atticus and Clare, no matter what. The mortgage must be paid, the car must have fuel in it and the fridge must be stocked. I must provide three hot meals for this young man for at least the next 20 years; with the invite to return to us forevermore.

Right now, I'm in a better financial position than I ever could have imagined. In part it's down to you buying this book (cheers), but it doesn't mean I'm not worried about what the future will bring. I've always said I must make as much money as I can as quickly as I can because my career as a comedian could last another ten years — or ten minutes, you just never know. In my game, people are cancelled every day. Careers are taken away in an instant, often over nothing (perhaps more than often). Will this continue through the decades? Who knows. It could get worse, it could get better.

The more I think about parenthood there's one fear that's worse than any other — the "what ifs". The "what ifs" always have and probably always will play a starring role in my life. When I was young, if Mum was late picking me up from school, I'd immediately ask myself . . . *what if she's dead?* That's how my mind works. As a comedian with 10 years' experience, just before I walk out on stage, I still go . . . *what if I'm not funny?* As a person with epilepsy, I can't help thinking . . . *what if I have a fit walking downstairs, in the car, or holding someone else's baby?*

But now I'm a dad-to-be . . . *what if something's wrong?*
What if something happens to Clare during the birth?
What if I'm a bad father?
What if I can't look after my family?
And on and on.

This fucking terrifies me more than anything. It keeps me awake at night and it puts my emotions and my stress responses into overdrive. It's mad to me to think that you can be so worried about something that you wake up the next day and actually feel the tension in your shoulders. That is how powerful thoughts can be. They can lead to pain in the muscles usually only reserved for the day after a massive session in the gym.

As much as we all hate it, at some level this anxiety can be quite healthy, as long as it doesn't dominate your existence. Believe it or not, the fear, the anxiety, the "what ifs", can help ground you and make you a better person. My anxiety has made me a nicer, happier and more caring man; hopefully a better father too. Sometimes it fucking sucks but it helps me get things done, makes me work harder, and keeps me focused.

The "what ifs" are like the devil and the angel on each of your shoulders, whispering into your ears. Picture, if you will, the 15th-century play *The Castle of Perseverance*, which popularised the idea of the good and bad angel, representing the two opposing forces in your inner monologue and personality. If you've never heard of *The Castle of Perseverance* don't worry, you're not alone. I just googled the origins of the good and bad shoulder angel and that popped up. I only included it to make me seem more intelligent than I am.

In one ear, the angel tells you that everything will be okay! But then without a moment to contemplate the newly found positive ideas, you learn from the devil in your other ear that everything is falling apart! Starting with you. It's the yin and yang of your emotional intelligence. It's necessary and horrifying simultaneously, but if you didn't have these voices you may be considered insane.

The "what ifs" are always playing on your mind. But for a soon-to-be parent everything, and I mean *everything*, is controlled by those fucking "what ifs". You have been told there is a baby in there but it's so small you can't see anything at this point. It looks nothing like a human and is only a few cells in size. You can't feel it, it can't hear you talking to it. It's all hypothetical and your hypothetical mind (your "what if" brain) takes over.

This is miserable, people.

A saying I have only recently come to understand is "misery loves company". I heard it as a child but never really got it, much like I never really got why people get so drunk on Christmas Day. Now I understand it perfectly: it's because they can't stand their families and to deal with the crazy they have to get blind (an Aussie term meaning "very drunk"). "Misery loves company" is perhaps the most accurate depiction of your surroundings when you're a parent-to-be. Friends, associates, the lady at the supermarket, work colleagues and randoms on the internet are going to lob in their two bob's worth. And two bob ain't worth shit. It's all negative. They're going to come for you and you will hear things like this . . .

"Say goodbye to sleep."

"You've *ruined* your life."

"You'll never have sex again!"

What's happening is these people are bringing the misery of *their* reality, borne of *their* shit attitude to parenthood or a relationship built on the age-old mindset of "you'll do". Their lives have fallen apart, and they see you with a smile on your face and they want to fucking break it. Parenthood is and always will be hard, but what in life that is so amazingly rewarding isn't? It's *all* fucking hard, so fucking what? If something is hard, to quote Jocko Willink, "Good." There is nothing I despise more than negative, pessimistic, sad people who try to bring others down to their level. In my mind that is reprehensible behaviour. As with anything in life worth doing, I accept the fact that being a dad will be hard. I understand there will be difficulties, sacrifices, reasons to be worried, to be scared and so much more. What makes a good mother or father is to accept it and face it head on.

What I never saw coming was how horribly affected your partner becomes during the first 12 weeks (the first trimester) of their pregnancy. Fatigue, morning sickness that lasts all day, cramps, terror, sadness, happiness, despair and everything in between. That's what your partner goes through and it's horrible. It all adds to your own anxiety and you can't help asking, did we do the right thing? And then there are the "what ifs" . . .

Brain chemistry is really fragile when you're pregnant. The closest women come to being pregnant before they are actually pregnant is being on birth control or "the pill". One thing I found out about the poor sheilas (Australian for "women") who are on the pill is that some actually fall in love while taking these exogenous hormones. But then after the wedding or honeymoon, when they quite commonly come off the pill, they find they are no longer attracted to their partner — in fact, they could be *repulsed* by the former love of their lives! This hypothesis was confirmed in a 2011 study[2] of 1514 women who didn't take the pill and 1005 who did. Those women who met their partner while on the pill experienced a massive drop in sexual satisfaction, sexual attraction and being up for new things in the boudoir when they stopped taking it. Which

2   www.ncbi.nlm.nih.gov/pmc/articles/PMC3282363

brings me to my conclusion: hormones in both fake pregnancy (the pill) and real life pregnancy are well and truly fucked.

This is why when a couple gets pregnant panic often sets in. Their brains are dealing with a huge uptick in chemicals. It's almost like there's a script pre-written for all women that they must recite during their pregnancy. And the man has to play along with this charade:

"I'm *so* excited."
"I can't wait to meet this bundle of joy."
"I've never been happier!"

You're supposed to be over the moon. And you *are*, but in the realm of "what ifs" you may not have these exact feelings immediately. Lots of mums-to-be feel bad about their mindset and themselves. It's this fucked-up, self-inflicted, unnecessary shame. It only makes you feel worse. And for the man, this helpless feeling engulfs your "what ifs". There are only so many times you can say "it's all going to be okay". It is a very stressful time for men, of that I have no doubt.

What doesn't help is that blokes don't understand shit. We are fucking hopeless, so women turn to their friends, parents and colleagues or, god forbid, Instagram, for help and guidance. But they are in on the charade as well . . .

"Oh, you must be *so* excited."
"You're going to be a great mum!"

But you are not. You are fucking terrified and now you start thinking you must be a bad mother because you're out of step with the pre-determined thought pattern. You're not playing the game you are supposed to believe and spruik for the next lot of girls and couples. One aspect of that game I really despise is that you shouldn't tell anyone for 12 weeks.

You may or may not be aware but when you find out you are pregnant, many folks — usually your parents — tell you to hold off sharing the news until you're three months in, just in case you lose the baby. Miscarriages are horrific experiences and many people deal with them throughout their lives. In fact, in Australia there are around 110,000 each year, and that's in a country of some 26 million people. In other parts of the world the numbers are much higher. Of the millions of women who become pregnant, many don't have the dream run – instead, they have the worst days of their lives. And it's not only them, their partners are affected as well. Miscarriage doesn't just floor the mother, it breaks the father in half too. The vast majority of those people who lost their baby were probably told at some point to "not tell anyone yet, it's too early" which leaves their family unit shattered and the parents-to-be feeling totally alone. There are many social conventions championed by our elders that belong in the past and this is without a doubt one of them.

Another great one, probably the most common, is the question: are you ready? It was actually something we constantly asked ourselves. Along with, is this the right move? Are we sure we want to flip our already pretty strange lives upside down? Is this a mistake? Will bringing a child into the world bring us closer together? Will we remain the same or, what scared me more than anything, will a kid fundamentally alter our relationship?

I'm sure you know plenty of older adults — maybe even your parents or grandparents — who at one point seemed very much in love, but somewhere along the line, something happened. Maybe it wasn't overnight, maybe it took a decade, but the foundations of the love they once shared became eroded and all they were left with was a mild hatred for one another. I couldn't imagine a worse outcome for two people in love. For Clare and me, a young couple, newly married, having a baby . . . would that happen to us? Was this the prophecy for all couples who have children, or were we going to be different?

As with most things in life, you're never really ready but that doesn't mean you should pull your dick out and scream, "No time like the present!" Get your shit together first. Get a decent job, make some money, get shelter. And be with someone you love and who loves you.

Regrettably, men and pregnancy just don't mix. There are far too many examples of us blokes getting someone pregnant and leaving, having the baby and leaving, or just not being there at all. Some men choose not to help their wives during pregnancy and then do the same when the baby arrives; others act like it's a burden. I'm here to tell you, that shit stops with me and with you.

Children need their fathers just as much as they need their mothers. I would argue they need them *more* at different times in their lives. At the beginning they need their mother, but during their early adulthood it is the father who becomes the most required voice and pillar of support.

The way men are treated during pregnancy and the things

we deal with are completely different to what our significant others face. To begin with, when your wife/girlfriend becomes pregnant they must contend with all manner of shit, from pain to fear and everything in between. They battle this stuff all day long. As Clare's pregnancy progressed I found myself becoming more and more frustrated that there was nothing I could do to help her. Sure, I could clean and cook, but she has to keep the pain and fear within herself. I imagine it's like having a loved one become very ill; you would do anything to take that pain for them, but there is nothing you can do. Then, after the baby arrives, your job doesn't stop. You are going to need to help her change bloody pads, help her on and off the toilet; you may even need to wipe her arse and if you are not willing to do that don't fucking get her pregnant! (By the by, Clare didn't require any arse wiping. She would be very upset if she knew you all thought I wiped her bum.)

As I say, men are second-class citizens during pregnancy. I get it, sort of, but I was still surprised to be treated by medical staff as a persona non grata — someone to be ignored and shunned. For example, throughout the pregnancy, you will attend appointments for ultrasounds, which will measure the size of your baby, and its development, and look for the horrible possibility of abnormalities. On our first visit, I went to walk inside and sit next to my wife in the waiting area. There I was met with a receptionist whom I can only imagine had a large stick up her arse. I was made aware that the waiting room was for mothers only and fathers had to wait down the hall.

It may seem trivial, but when you experience this whole, terrifying process from the backseat, it only cements the fact delivered to us by our history that as a man you *do not matter.* That is bullshit and it needs to change. We as men must be our wives'/girlfriends'/partners' number one support in this situation; in fact, in *all* situations. Men get a bad rap because of the deeds done by our fathers and our fathers' fathers. It is up to us to reset the standards and dictate how we will be defined in the future. In reality, this is all about legacy; it's about how we will be remembered. That may sound cheesy, but at the end of the day, our job is to improve the lives of our children and our partners. To make them stronger. We must set the example so they know we're going provide, protect and love them better than anyone who has ever done it before.

Gentlemen, this is your challenge.

—

The day my son was born started like any other. Our dog Littlefoot (named after the dinosaur in the *The Land Before Time*) woke us up to go to the toilet — his "midnight shit" as we call it. He was a little late this morning, it was 2.30 am, but I got up anyway. Our other dog Rosie was awake too, so I assumed she wanted to go out as well. But then she immediately sat back down. A bit strange, but she was an elderly dog so sometimes she would, like an old lady, do some interesting things.

So I took Littlefoot outside, and seconds later I heard Clare yell from the bathroom. I rushed back inside and found her standing up doing what only can be described as "leaking".

Perhaps "leaking" is an understatement — water was *spewing* from her "below area" like the possessed girl in *The Exorcist*. We looked at each other, freaked the fuck out then panicked some more before we agreed that her waters had broken.

Daylight savings had ended at 3 am that morning so the clocks were wound back and we arrived at the hospital at about 2.45 am. Before we left for the hospital, just as the doctor had asked, I had to do something important. Shave Clare's pubes. After all the stress and anxiety it was hilarious. Picture us in the bathroom at 2 am, me on my knees, shaving my heavily pregnant wife with my beard trimmer, literally moments after her water had broken. But I did what had to be done, and when we arrived at the hospital, we were lucky enough to have a lovely midwife take care of us. She ran us through the birth plan and told us that we'd likely be heading in for a C-section at about 8 am.

In those final hours before becoming a dad, I sat there thinking about all the things Clare and I had done as a couple. There was so much I enjoyed and was immensely proud of. We had ticked so much off peoples' lifetime bucket lists at a relatively young age, which gave me the confidence to know that I was absolutely ready to become Dad and Clare was more than ready to become Mum.

I know many expecting parents see the final months, weeks, days or hours before their baby is born as the last time they'll ever be alone again. I thought of it in a similar way, but most of those people see that as a negative, it didn't even cross my mind. I was born to be a Dad and Clare was born to be a Mum. We understood the terror of what was to come but we had never been more ready for anything in our entire lives.

Sure enough, around 8 am it was time, and we were wheeled down the corridor to the theatre. Just before we went through the doors the anaesthetist stopped me in the hallway. He asked me to wait — apparently I needed a hairnet (for my head but not my beard). The nurse took forever to come and because there was so much riding on all of this — the life of my child and the life of the love of my life, mixed with a huge amount of excitement — I just burst into tears. The surgeon whom we'd become friends with over the past nine months appeared at that point, calmed me down, assured me that everything would be all right and led me into theatre.

—

If I'm being perfectly honest, the birth was *horrible*. The spinal block (given to the patient to stop them feeling pain below a certain level) wasn't strong enough in our opinion and Clare spent some of the surgery, particularly towards the end, screaming in pain. But all of that was forgotten when halfway through, they pulled down the curtain and there he was, our little man, our son, Atticus. We embraced for the first time as a family — a moment I'll never forget — and time stopped. Blood, tears, crying — what a moment! Atti was very quiet but thankfully, as moments went by, he became more and more lively. I held onto my wife and son, not really knowing what was going on. It scared the shit out of me.

Clare had bled a lot, but they got things under control,

stitched her up and I was sent off to wait for her in recovery. I sat there with Atti, my first time alone with him. I had to stop staring at him because once again I couldn't stop crying. It was just pure love. It was the same feeling I had on my wedding day looking into my wife's eyes.

—

That night, after the visitors, the new uncles, aunties and grandparents had all left, Clare and I sat there and just watched our son Atti, looking longingly at the perfect little person we'd made. We had never been prouder and both agreed that yes, this would be hard and of course, we were anxious about how this would change our lives, but we were absolutely sure it was the best decision we had ever made. Our goal is to raise our son to become a loving, kind, gentle and compassionate person, a hard-working, driven and brave man, and one day a protective, intelligent and loyal husband and father. We will take him everywhere and we will show him what is possible if you are willing to work for it.

Bringing a child into the world is the hardest decision a man or woman will ever have to make. If you fuck it up, you'll ruin a life. So do not make this decision lightly. Make sure you're with the right person because if you are, it will forever change your life and make you happier, prouder and more in love than you could ever imagine.

Chapter 7: **Small wins**

"The secret of all victory lies in the organisation of the non-obvious." — *Marcus Aurelius*

WINNING ISN'T everything. We've all heard the saying, right? In a world of "participation trophies" and pats on the back for doing fuck all, we've all been programmed to think that just showing up is going to cut it. Okay, it's nice and whatnot, but it also teaches us that we have succeeded even when in reality we literally have achieved nothing. This rewards us and allows us, subconsciously at least, for the rest of our lives, to expect praise and happiness *immediately*. Well, I'm sorry, but waiting for that dopamine drip like a thirsty hamster on a hot day breaks people. It's really that bad. Receiving accolades during childhood any time we just show up, even if we don't put in the work, even if we don't work hard, even if we don't win, destroys more people than it helps.

We're told these lies very early on. I guess your parents or teachers, whoever it was who told you this, sort of had a point. You don't have to be a dick about winning at *everything*; it's nice to share and all that bullshit. But as an adult, when it's no longer about letting little Timmy win because he'll cry — it's now about your actual existence — if you're not properly winning at least some of the time, then your life is going to suck. As adults, it's no longer a kids' ball game; it's paying the bills; it's paying the mortgage; it's finding a partner; it's getting a decent job. Lose at those things and you'll start to realise that winning *is* everything. If you disagree, ask anyone on the street — the downtrodden — if winning is important. You won't like the answer.

I know we have all seen the bullshit videos of people who have achieved nothing in their lives but sell their terrible life-coaching PDFs and whatnot to desperate people. They love telling you that you must win, but that doesn't fucking mean anything really. They don't know what they are talking about. They are just giving empty advice, devoid of substance. They haven't even done the things they are trying to sell, so please, in this chapter, know that I have put into play every last thing I am talking about., I have lived each experience. I may not have all the answers but at least I gave this a crack for myself — and it worked.

Many of us, if not every last human on Earth, with the capacity to think freely, can dream, can desperately believe that one day they will achieve something, something that is magical, something that completes us and our seemingly meaningless existence. Unfortunately, in the same way that we are programmed not to focus on winning at a young age, we are also taught that dreams, hopes and wants are for children. We're told that grown-ups shouldn't even entertain that shit, and this is what breaks people. We're told that in order to fit in with the mundane experience most of the people around us share, you have to give up.

Hopes and dreams aren't overly complicated things. When we're kids, they start off simply. "I want to get big." In our infancy, we have no clue that for most of us growth is inevitable and we will very soon achieve the dream of being "big" like Mum and Dad — we don't even have to try! The desperation that is built into the human baby to grow up is puzzling. Many of us look back on our younger years as the best time of our lives, so why is it written into human nature that we are desperate to move on from this stage? I believe it's some kind of ancient advice written into our DNA, for without it we don't grow, or spread our wings, leave the nest or catch the worm in the early morning, whichever bird metaphor you prefer.

Like a giraffe, we humans are hurrying to grow and fend for ourselves. But the huge difference between a human being and an African animal is that a giraffe is born on bare dirt and grass and has only moments to get its bearings and instantly grow up. If it fails to do this, it'll become breakfast for the predators lurking in the morning mist.

Human beings don't just have moments; we have the best part of two decades to leave the nest, sort our shit out and get on in the real world. And yet, almost as though our ancestors are speaking through us, we cannot wait to grow up. Maybe this is epigenetics or maybe this is just the human condition. We all want what we don't have. Whatever it may be, it motivates us, it drives us and we're possessed by it even when we don't need it, like our bodies growing from babies to toddlers. The first few years are full of unfortunately flexible necks and the shittiest of shitty nappies. In this period we learn how to get what we want, vomit, crawl and that boobs are just plain wonderful.

This is why we are not given permission biologically to remember the trauma of early childhood. Imagine having a memory in your mind right this second of being pushed with great exertion, feeling pain and terror, out your poor mother's birth canal. Or suckling at your mum's teat for hours on end. What a horrifying image. (For most of us, at least. Insert your countries' area of most incestuous populace here; Tasmanians excluded, of course.) Everything we do in those early years is by instinct or forced on us by our parents. Although you may not remember it, it's at this point in your life that you are beginning to form your opinions of the world and develop the flavour palette for what you want and what you enjoy. As we grow, our dreams follow suit. They change from "I want to be big" to "I want to be a firefighter", "a dancer", "a dinosaur", then "I want to be a doctor". They may sound very different to the dreams of a tiny infant, but they are not. These are dreams of becoming something more, something different to what you are now, something bigger; progressing.

Dreams have to be amazing and breathtaking. As youngsters our dreams are always something unfeasible, but as we age they become more and more realistic until they dwindle to "I hope I have enough money to retire in 40 years" and "I really hope I can pay the mortgage this week". How fucking depressing is that? Surely something is wrong with the way we think and operate when we can go from believing anything is possible to dreaming about not being homeless. Your real dream, in its most virtuous form, is always something grand, something beautiful; it expresses your innermost passions, beliefs and genetic code.

Ask a six year old why she wants to be a doctor and it's not because of the good remuneration. She doesn't care about the 14 years in university and the crippling debt she will incur. No, she just wants to help people. Our dreams are pure but, regrettably, life will do everything it can to crush whatever you set your mind to.

From the baby wanting to being big, to the 10 year old wanting to put out fires, we move to the teenager who, it is my melancholy duty to inform you, now for some reason begins to give up on every dream they ever had. Which is sad, but could you think of a more shared experience across the human population? "I guess it's just not going to happen for me." We have all thought that about one thing or another and just decided to settle. It's heartbreaking that somehow from the ages of 0 to 13, a baby with all the potential in the world — literally with the world at their feet — can, for all intents and purposes, just give up.

How does this happen? Why do people give in to the struggle so easily?

The American author Steven Pressfield coined a term for

this: "resistance". He believes resistance is the most significant force in the human life cycle. It stops you from doing pretty much anything you know you want to do. In his book *The War of Art*, which I highly recommend, he explains how resistance hinders every creative person. It stops you writing. It fills you full of thoughts like "I'll do it later". It stops the painter painting. "It's too cold." "My hands are too stiff to hold the brush this morning." But I think resistance affects absolutely everyone — not just the creatives. The hopeful bodybuilder, the jiu-jitsu white belt, the comedian, the business owner, the entrepreneur; everyone faces it and this is why so many people give in and give up. Resistance gives you the way out. It provides immediate relief and makes giving up easy. Stopping and retreating is seductive because you don't have to try. It gives you instant gratification and a fleeting feeling of success. You get a little rush of dopamine and that cements the likelihood of you just giving up next time.

Resistance doesn't seem to be something we really listen to as children though. Something happens in the teenage and young adult years when this innate philosophy that drives us to always dream bigger and move forward, withers and dies. I think everyone is to blame for this, but school in particular is terrible.

"Hey kids, what do you want to be when you grow up?"
"A musician!"
"I want to save the world!"
"I want to go to the Olympics!"
Or what I said, "I want to be a comedian!"
A lot of teachers, maybe because their hopes and dreams

were crushed long ago, meet these responses with, "It's time to grow up", or "Think about what you're going to study at university" — which is ridiculous for a 17 or 18 year old who can barely stop wanking let alone decide what they want to do for the rest of their lives. Teachers believe because it didn't happen for them, it won't happen for you. They have been infected by Pressfield's "resistance" and they are fucking super spreaders.

Humans are conditioned to survive by any means necessary. Maybe that's why as youngsters our minds are malleable to our environment. But we are also given strict instructions by the very fibre of our being to take the path of least resistance. It's when we start doing this that we form the bad habits that will follow us into adulthood and kill our dreams right in front of our very eyes. Our culture right now programs young people — and all of us at some point — to *just give up*. If something is going wrong in your life, it's someone else's fault.

It's the safe spaces.

It's the equality of outcomes.

It's the fairytale world where everyone is special.

The forced diversity.

Rewarding weakness.

It's the fucking participation trophies!

None of this is about being an alpha male or any of that shit. If you call yourself an alpha male I guarantee you, you will suck all the dicks in the world. And it has nothing to do with gender; this applies to girls and women as well. This is about humans looking for the easy way out and our society feeding it to them on a plastic spoon; not even a metal spoon, a soft plastic spoon so as to not damage delicate tooth enamel.

So, now you realise that all your dreams are going to fail, your life will fall apart, you will never be anything you expected, and everyone hates you, especially me. What can you do from here?

Well, I'll let you in on a little secret: life is all about the small wins. It is about the tortoise and the hare. It all started with the ancient Greek fable that was passed down by word of mouth, and it's seen countless reiterations over the centuries. Almost every society and culture has a version. In French it's called *Le Lièvre et la Tortue*. In Latin, *De Lepore et Testudine*. In the early part of the 20th century, Irish writer Lord Dunsany focused less on the speed of the race but on the journey. The tortoise's shell was a metaphor for a hard life, "hard shell hard living". Perhaps it was the life experience that helped the tortoise beat the over-aroused hare (aroused meaning excited, not erect, although I do believe running with an erection would be difficult, perhaps pole vault would be your sport, or darts, depending on the size of your member). Regardless of which tale is most familiar to you, the message is the same:

> The tortoise and the hare face each other in a race. The hare takes a great lead, so great it has a nap along the road. The slow but steady tortoise sneaks past the sleeping hare and wins the race. The hare is probably skinned and made into a stew while the tortoise has a coke-fuelled party and fucks a stripper (slowly). Otherwise known as "the dream".

Meaning, at least in my mind, that it's not who gets off to the best start. It doesn't even matter how the race goes or how you finish. All that matters is *finishing*.

—

You meet plenty of people when you're younger who have had a better start than you. They may continue in this vein for some time. It may be financially, academically or sexually — some of our peers just do better than us. However, early success can very well be your undoing. Tragically those who find early success often reach failure quicker. Why? They stop trying. Think of the kids you went to school with who were the best at sport at a young age. Chances are they aren't playing professionally now. It was too easy, they didn't try and, like the hare, the tortoises overtook them eventually.

Remember the best-looking guys or girls in your year at school, the stunner of each gender? Where are they now? The guy is probably doing a job he hates, drinking his sorrows away with a family he despises because he couldn't pull out in time. The girl meanwhile is married to a wanker who drinks too much and jizzed in her, and now she's stuck with Karly and Kyle. Her morning begins with anti-psychotics and ends with Moscato. Every day she thinks, *Where did the good years go?* And then there's the rest of us — the ugly ones — look at us, we are fucking killing it! Unless you're still ugly, then well, take this book back to where you bought it and get a refund, you are beyond help.

Failure is a wonderful thing. You learn so much from it.

The American inventor Thomas Edison was once asked how many times he had made a woman orgasm. His response? "None, but I've found 48 ways *not* to make a woman orgasm." I may have fucked that saying up, but you get the drift. The point is if you fail, you either try again, or you give up. Those are your only options.

I'm friends with two young and extremely popular celebrities (who will remain nameless) who built huge platforms on YouTube before they even left high school. It is my fear that because they have never had real jobs or known what it is like to struggle, to work shit jobs, to do it tough, that they will fail in the end. This has nothing to do with their talent — it's about the fact that they went straight from high school to fame and a job that pays $10K+ a week. They're doing very well for themselves right now, but how will they fair in a decade? Only time will tell.

I worked every shit job you can imagine. I delivered pizzas, I installed shower screens, I worked on building sites, in security, in a warehouse, as a landscaper — the list goes on and on. I hated pretty much every one of those jobs. They were hard; not so much physically, but mentally. Every day you'd drag yourself out of bed to go somewhere you loathed. You did it for 38 hours a week, wishing you were back at school, only to get paid on a Thursday, piss half your paycheque up the wall by Friday, and throw the rest in "where's the gold" on Saturday. But all of those shit jobs taught me something important. I learnt about a "baseline" — a starting point. I learnt that if I gave up, then this was the life I was destined to have.

I knew I needed a change, but the question was, how the fuck do I achieve my dream? The dream I'd had since I was a kid. The one that had been programmed out of me and replaced with some shit university degree that meant nothing but being in debt. That is where my love for the idea of "small wins" came from. I knew I wanted to be a comedian, but something my father instilled in me at a young age is not only that you must have a goal, but you must also have *incremental goals* on the way that build towards your overall success.

"I want to be a professional comedian" was something I said a lot. But really what I really should have been saying is:

- I'm going to study comedy
- I'm going to understand timing
- I'm going to make time to write
- Write two minutes of material
- Practise two minutes of material
- Write five minutes of material
- Practise five minutes of material
- Procrastinate
- Find a venue to do an open mic
- Shit pants
- Do an open mic
- Do well
- Rearrange and re-rewrite your five minutes of material
- Repeat for five years
- Create a YouTube channel
- Put two to three videos out each week

- Repeat for a year
- Then another two years
- Get enough followers to do a tour
- Shit pants because you only have five minutes of material and have never done an hour-long show
- Write 10 minutes of material
- Do an open mic
- Write 20 minutes of material
- Do an open mic
- Repeat
- Get on stage
- You are now a professional comedian

If I had become a professional comedian after my first step I would not be here. If I started my career on TikTok and rocketed to fame, I would not be here. This apprenticeship of doing shit, failing, bombing, writing and repeating was so important; it laid the foundation that I stand on to this day. It's so necessary to have a stable base because without it, at some point, you will crumble. There is only so long you can pretend to be something that you are not. Eventually you will be found out and that's why doing the work is so fucking important. This approach and mindset can be moulded to anything you want to achieve in this world.

Have your goal, then break down step by step how you will do it, and celebrate the small wins on the way, because you are fucking doing it. You're not just sitting there saying I want this, or I'm going to be that, *you are fucking doing it.*

If I didn't break things down step by step I would not

be here. I did exactly this to create a YouTube following. In the beginning I started out posting mainly to Facebook and then occasionally YouTube (I eventually stopped Facebook because I kept getting banned).

For both platforms this was my plan:

1. The first step was to make videos about extremely niche topics. I made them about my home town of Newcastle; jokes about the city. The aim of this was to bring in the audience that related to that humour, get them to follow, and then I had them.
2. The next step was to make videos about my state. This was done by making videos about State of Origin, a sporting event which is massive in New South Wales and Queensland, bringing in those followers.
3. The last step was trying to suck everyone in from all over Australia. So I made videos about people talking shit about Australia, not liking the food, not understanding the culture. All of these things led to the most viral traction. I still have people coming up to me and saying, "You're that guy who gave me 10 reasons not to visit Australia!" and yes, yes I did. I've also made nearly 1000 other videos since then; maybe catch up with my uploads, you fuck.

But my plan to draw people in worked. I started small and grew exponentially over time.

I truly believe that if you have a goal or a dream you have to chase it, but don't just run after it with your arms flailing and your eyes closed. Get a plan and work out exactly *how* you are going to do it. Every successful human being didn't just get where they are instantly. They had countless small wins along the way and I'm not just talking about successful business people or sportsmen or women, I'm talking about great parents, positive thinkers and, more importantly, happy people. I am here and you are reading my words because, like the tortoise, I know this is a game of small wins and in the very end enough small wins will allow you to achieve anything. Don't let your natural human drive, your motivation, die alongside your childhood innocence. Don't let people take that from you. Fucking dream and fucking make it work for you.

Just because your parents or your teachers couldn't do it, doesn't mean you won't. Maybe you feel trapped? Maybe you have kids and a mortgage and your dream is out of reach. Okay, I still think you could do it but it's going to take a lot of sacrifice and if you're not willing to do that, then you look yourself in the eyes tonight, stare into the mirror and you make sure your kids believe in themselves and their dreams. Tell them about the small wins, explain to them that's how they are going to get there. That's how they are going to win!

Be the tortoise. Be the one willing to put their weird penis-like neckhead down and do the fucking work.

Chapter 8: **Marry your best friend**

IF THERE is one piece of advice about love and relationships I want to give you, it is this: marry your best friend. I'm sure you've heard the expression before. But maybe you've never really given it much thought. Maybe you think you're too young to worry about it now, and maybe you are, but how many people in their thirties or forties are married? Most of them. And that's probably going to be you sooner or later. So read this chapter very carefully otherwise you will fuck it all up.

Regardless of your position in life, think about it like this: on average when you are in a committed relationship you will spend upwards of three hours with your significant other every single day. You will wake up next to them, go to sleep next to them, eat with them. Everything you do, they will be right by your side and if you marry them, chances are this will go on for quite a long time. You might assume the average marriage lasts around 40 years, right? But here's the kicker: in Australia, based on 2019 data, the average marriage is just over *12 years*. That's right, each year, in a country of only 26 million people, there are around 50,000 divorces. In America, with its much bigger population, there are almost 1,000,000 divorces a year! So many people are fucking up their relationships and that is why you should care and heed my warning that all of this can be avoided if you just marry your best friend.

When I say your "best friend", here's what I'm *not* saying. Don't marry someone you get along well with. Don't marry someone you tolerate. Don't marry someone just because they are hot. Don't fucking marry someone because it's easy, or because you have been together long enough now and you *have* to marry them — *no, no, no!* Marry someone who is honestly your best mate. The one person you need to be around, someone who understands you and would do anything for you. Someone you will be as in love with now in their youth, as you will be when they're an old decrepit grandma (or grandpa) shitting themselves and refusing to put the air conditioner on when its 45 fucking degrees outside.

Ask yourself these hard questions about your prospective spouse:

Do they actually love you?
Do you actually love them?
Would they give you their last dollar?

Do they care more about your happiness than their own?

Would they give their life for you?

I know it might seem like we've taken a detour to drama town, but this is someone you are going to spend every day with for the rest of your life, so you better not fuck it up.

You will quickly discover in the dating world — whether you're 18 or mid-twenties or older — that pretty much everyone is insane. No, seriously, people are fucking mental and this is why, like you, they are single. I know this from personal experience. I have dated all kinds of strange humans. There was one girl who knew I had no money but demanded I take her to the most expensive restaurant in Newcastle. I couldn't afford two mains so she got a main and I got an entrée and then she ate fucking half of my entrée. Safe to say that one lasted a very short time. She also used to sing aloud in my parent's house when she came over and it did everyone's fucking head in. I broke up with her over the phone; dick move, but I'm proud of it.

I also dated a girl who got absolutely blind drunk after a few drinks and carried on like an idiot, running around screaming, lying on the ground, pretending to be drunker than she actually was. She'd then proceed to spew everywhere. This happened any time she drank, by the way. And how could I forget the girl who told me out of the blue one night, "Jesus is more important than this relationship." That was different. We weren't even talking about religion at this point. Fucking weirdo.

I've been there and done that, unfortunately quite literally.

The Tinder dates, the first dates, getting stood up, realising they are insane, heartbreak, saying dumb shit, trying to pick up girls in nightclubs and failing miserably. I have experienced it all and that's very important. If you're thinking, *I've never experienced crazy, I don't know what he's talking about, I met the girl of my dreams straight away,* she *is* the crazy one, mate. Fucking watch out.

I even had a girl pull a weapon on me. Not in an aggressive way, but it was terrifying nonetheless. One cold lonely evening I drove about 40 minutes to meet a girl I matched with on Tinder. Now I know that sounds pretty sad but one of my mates once drove from Newcastle to Tamworth, about three hours, just for a booty call. So I was sad but not that sad. Anyway, we drove around for a bit and then ended up parking near the beach and having something to eat. Then a question popped into my mind about safety, which may have come across as creepy but I was genuinely interested. I asked her, "You don't know me, I could be a murderer. How do you keep safe in this situation?"

"Oh, with this," she replied and proceeded to pull the biggest knife I've ever seen on a woman out of her Ugg boot. Yes, her Ugg boot. I know, I know, I should have known. Random girl, Ugg boots, I was on the Central Coast, so many alarm bells. (The knife was a bowie knife, think *Crocodile Dundee*.) As the famous saying goes, "It's hard to get hard, with a knife in her boot." I think it was Plato who said that.

This wasn't my only trip down the freeway from Newcastle to meet up with someone. One night I organised a meeting with a girl I'd matched with on Tinder. Once again, shameful,

I know, but I was 20, what can you do? I was pretty prolific on Tinder. In fact, I got so good at it that I had a message I would send to every girl I matched with. It sat in my Notes app on my phone and I would copy and paste it every single time. It read:

"Hi, thank you for your interest,

"Unfortunately, Isaac has received the limit on matches one account can receive per week. We would like to apologise for this inconvenience, I know you must be devastated, better luck next time."

Personally, I thought it was hilariously imaginative, but in reality, I don't think it ever actually worked.

Anyway, I planned to meet this chick at 10 pm. She lived maybe an hour away from my house but I told her I lived 45 minutes in the *opposite* direction so we agreed to meet in the middle, which is actually only about 10–15 minutes from my house — absolute genius. We parked at this car park — it was the dodgiest situation — I flashed my car headlights, she flashed hers and she got out and started walking over.

I know this sounds horrible, but she lied to me because the photos she used on Tinder were, let's say, highly edited. In real life she was big, I'm talking fucking huge, the white whale from *Moby Dick*. She was fat, yes, but even more alarmingly, she was tall, maybe six foot five inches, and would have weighed more than me. Now, I'm a very polite man, as we have established, so I switched on my car as she approached. She must have thought, *How nice, he's putting the air conditioner on.* Fuck that, I drove out of there like my life fucking depended on it. It was like a scene from a disaster movie starring Dwayne "the Rock" Johnson; the world was crumbling down behind me, but thank the lord I got out just in time. Of course I felt bad, but a few hours later she sent me a video of her deep-throating a dildo stuck to her bathtub with the caption, "This could have been you". She also slapped herself in the face with it. Some gals, hey.

I did date some genuinely good people, some not so good, but more importantly than anything, I learnt a lot about women, dating and growing up. "Growing up" is key here. You do a lot of that in your late teens and into your twenties so be careful whom you choose to spend time with because over a decade you can, and probably will, become a very different person. Let's be honest; if you're the same person at 28 as you were at 18 you are without a shadow of a doubt a fuckwit and you need to sort your life out.

This may offend some people, but here's another lesson I need you to know.

Marrying your first love — that first boyfriend or girlfriend out of high school or, worse, the boyfriend or girlfriend you met and started dating *in* high school — is the dumbest idea of all time. Not only are you a very different person from when you met that person to when you sign that piece of paper saying you'll be with them *forever*, you're basically still a kid and you're only together because you met in school and it's easy.

On that, don't just sleep with one person and then dust your hands and say, "They'll do." If you only date one person then you're probably going to get to the age of 24 and think, *Fuck, I wouldn't mind doing some nasty extracurricular fucking.* We all know people like this. I saw it in high school with the kids who went to religious youth groups. Forty-five seconds after they graduated they married the boy or girl their parents picked for them and then *boom*, a few years later, they all got divorced.

It isn't nice to say, but you have to test the waters. You never mount the first fish that you catch; what if it's a shitty squid or a toadfish? Get back out there, put some better bait on your line and catch that marlin. (I mean "mount" as in put on the wall like a trophy fish, not sex BTW.)

Many relationships fail after marriage because you simply just don't know the person. Think back to your parents or your grandparents; how many of them got married before they lived together or really spent any time with each other? They dated once a week and then before you know it, Mum's been cream-pied and they think, *Fuck, better get married . . .*

Living together is crucial. It may be the best test for a relationship and, can I just add, you need to do it for a while, a long while. It's all very well going on a date with someone, the problem is on a date they're usually the very best version of themselves. They tell you how good they are, how wonderful their dreams are, and they spend the whole night trying to impress you; it's all an act. Living together is a whole other story. You actually get to be around them when they're at their worst, at their laziest and in their downtime. This is when we learn the most about a person. We find the things we like, dislike, love and cannot stand, but if they're your perfect person, you probably won't find many negative things, if any.

If you're thinking about getting married and signing a contract saying "I'll be yours forever and if we change our minds you can have half my stuff", then think really bloody hard. If you can't stand spending the weekend with them, don't fucking marry them, dickhead.

The perfect partner makes sacrifices for you. We are all different people at the end of the day and it is rare to share all the same interests, beliefs, likes and dislikes, so you may have to make changes to how you live for each other. Lots of women say "I'm not changing for a man" and men say the same thing. Well, dickheads, you may never be truly happy. If a couple is willing to make sacrifices for each other, it becomes a counterbalance, their sacrifice makes up for yours and yours for theirs and happiness is often the result.

So many relationships are based just on rooting (sex) and I get it. Sex is good, it's great, and I've even done it a few times, but it's not the only part of a solid relationship. Any idiot can have sex, just drive past your local (insert low socio-economic area here) and you'll see a whole heap of offspring that never should have been shot out of anywhere or into anyone. Actually, that's unfair, there are plenty of shit people in affluent areas, if not more.

On the topic of offspring, here's an idea: don't pump out as many kiddies as humanly possible and then wonder why you and your partner hate each other. I know many couples who had a baby, were so happy, smitten, in love, and then had the bright idea of pumping out another one when their first was only a few years old. "Oh, he/she has to have a little friend to play with." Let them be friends with, I dunno, kids their own age, from school or in your street. Who the fuck wants to play with their siblings? What happens to the parents with a few kids under five? They barely see each other and when they do they are too tired to do anything fun together. This compounds per baby over time and all of a sudden you're living with a fat angry stranger you for some reason married 30 years ago. Fuck that.

There is nothing wrong with having a *few* kids, that's not what I'm saying. All I'm suggesting is you take it case by case. You do not have to have a huge tribe of children, you can just have one. Maybe that suits your relationship better; each to their own.

You must also ask yourself, when this person is old and grey, and all the kids have moved out, could I follow them as they walk slowly to the shops on pension day letting farts out between steps? If, once the attraction fades you don't love them as much, then you are royally fucked. This is why marrying your best friend is everything.

But you can't force it.

At the end of the day, the connection you have, create — and then work on — is paramount. There has to be a connection, a *real* connection. If they are "the one", a good test is this: post-coitus, do you want to get as far away from each other as humanly possible? You also won't dread heading home from work to see them; you won't be terrified of the weekend or being at home alone with them, and you probably won't be itching to get out of the house with your mates any chance you get.

For some of you, that last paragraph may have reminded you of your own life. If so, I'm sorry to say you made a mistake. Your time at work, away, at the gym, should, if she's your best friend, be spent thinking, *I'm looking forward to getting home and seeing her.* I'm not suggesting you should be obsessed with someone, but also I am: I'm obsessed with my wife Clare. A healthy obsession can be good, it's not necessary, just you probably do not want to dry heave when their name is mentioned. That's a sign it's not going too well.

Clare is the best thing that's ever happened to me. We spend every hour of every day together and if you just read that and shuddered a little, thinking, *I'd hate to be around my husband or wife, boyfriend or girlfriend that much*, then maybe they are not your perfect match. I have no doubt Clare and I are each other's soul mates. If there is a person on this earth you are supposed to meet, then she is mine and I am hers. Over the years, we have slowly and hilariously morphed into the same person. We act like pensioners now. If we don't eat by 6 pm we freak out, bedtime is at 10, we watch *Midsomer Murders* together with cups of English breakfast tea, and I'm not interested in a world without her. Our relationship comes first, before everything; the rest of my family, my job, what I want to do with my career, my health. Clare comes first! Now with Atticus here that has changed — he is on par with her, but nothing trumps her.

We have never had a fight. We have argued, disagreed, maybe even gotten a little shitty, but a fight, no way. I'm not going to fight with my wife. I'm here to protect and support her, not argue with her. It is a great failure of humankind that fighting between couples, sometimes every single day, has become normalised. What a horrible way to live your life, battling with the one person who should be your rock. I'm sure the vast majority of us had parents who fought. This could be for dozens of reasons or just a few. Whatever the case, most domestic skirmishes can be remedied with simple communication. Unfortunately, some people of generations past (and even now) just cannot talk through their problems.

Talk to each other, you idiots!

I'm not sure when the concept that couples fight became the norm, whether it's from years past and built into the epigenetics of our romantic code, or maybe it's just because it is easy to fight with the one closest to you. Human beings are addicted to the path of least resistance and we look for it everywhere. We want it in business, at the gym, eating, cooking, anywhere we can avoid something hard, and maybe that's why we fight with our partners. It's not normal to yell at your wife — well maybe it is normal, but there is no way it should be. If you find yourself fighting with your loved one, or perhaps beyond your loved ones, know this: this world is bigger than you! Your partner and their wellbeing, alongside that of your children, is more important than you! This is all part of being a man and you should learn that this fucking second.

Once you realise this, everything else makes sense. You are playing a game and this game is like a great puzzle constantly moving and changing directions. If you can just sit back and love the people you are around — and I mean really love them — then it feels like you have the cheat codes, everything goes smoother, you can see every move in front of you. Fighting doesn't exist.

It may seem as if you are just crumbling, being subservient to your partner and doing everything for everyone else, well, that's where your partner picks up the slack. You help them in areas they need help and vice versa. Voilà! Happy couple. But you have to be willing to make the sacrifices.

Some people are already in turmoil when it comes to the relationship with their loved one and sometimes when given the obvious advice of "talk to them", their response is that he/she won't talk to me or they can't communicate, they don't sacrifice. Well, I'm sorry, but to be blunt, you didn't marry your best friend and there's not much more you can do.

I'll never forget meeting Clare . . . It was late one Sunday night, maybe around 11 pm. I was out on the town with one of my great mates, Jacque. Jacque was known all across the land as a bit of a loose unit. Anyway, we spent the afternoon from about 4 pm drinking cheap Coronas at the Prince in Newcastle, which was, back then, the spot to go on a Sunday. Then after it hit about 8 pm everyone who was anyone (young people or unemployed people, I think at this time I was both) would make the journey in a rickety old courtesy bus to the King Street Hotel, which wasn't the grossest nightclub in Australia but it was up there. Jacque and I had a couple of double Blacks, checked out the local talent (they checked us out too, with disgust) and after a few hours we wandered over the road to the 24/7 McDonald's. If you're thinking that's got to be the most unlikely venue for meeting the love of one's life, think again. For there, sitting out the front, sipping an iced coffee and waiting for her mum and dad to pick her up, was my future wife.

Naturally, Jacque made the first approach, creeping her out more than humanly possible. But I soon arrived and saved the day, a drunk knight in shining armour (I was actually wearing a green shirt with flamingos on it). If I never made that approach my life would have been very different. I don't even want to think about it. And Clare's life might have been worse. It could have been a Stephen King horror story — she could have ended up with Jacque! — a point she made at our wedding when we mentioned this part of our origin story and she yelled out to Jacque, "Could have been you, mate!"

At this point in my life, I'd just started doing comedy. I'd been doing open mics and had done three or four actual shows as a guest, one of which I'd filmed and posted to my personal Facebook page. It got a few likes from friends, but one total stranger saw it and really liked it and believe it or not that was Clare, the very same 19-year-old girl sitting out the front of Maccas late on a Sunday night. I found this out when she said to me, "You're a comedian, aren't you?" Yes I was. As horrifying as it sounds, I married my first fan. Something I'd probably get cancelled for now.

Clare is the funniest person I've ever known; no one makes me laugh like her. She has written some of the best jokes I've ever told on stage. I'm pretty sure one that I've been cancelled for was hers, but I'll claim it. We have some of the best and most outrageous conversations of all time, we talk all manner of shit, and we make fun of everyone. Clare does brilliant impressions, her timing is impeccable, she should do stand-up and I remind her of that constantly.

Knowing that someone can make you laugh at all times and in all situations can really calm your nerves about what the future will hold for your relationship. It doesn't matter what we'll look like when we're 80 (I'm sure she will be beautiful then of course), because if you have laughter that fills your day every day, then happiness will remain forever.

Beauty is something Clare has in abundance, but the main reason I married her is because of her kindness. She puts everyone else before herself and would run into oncoming traffic to save a stray dog — much to my constant dismay when she tries to get out of the car on the highway; but that's beautiful her. She will stop to sit and talk with homeless people. She was the first girlfriend I ever had who took the time to actually engage with my brother, Rory. She didn't see his autism as a reason to just say hello from afar, she wanted to get to know him.

Over the years Clare encouraged/demanded we rescue three amazing dogs. Actually, she demanded we rescue more but I had to, as the oldest, tell her to calm the fucking farm, the farm she was trying to build. It was with our first two dogs, Rosie and Littlefoot, and other animals in the years prior, that I learnt just what an amazing mother she would be. I was already reasonably confident from how brilliantly she treated me, but to see her with those animals, it was cemented as fact.

Clare saved me when it came to my mental health issues. She helped me navigate the worst and was able to do so because she'd had her own struggles. She was tested as a child and almost broken from all angles; she had a very tough childhood. Without it and without her knowledge, I don't know if I would be here. She has been for many years, and continues to be, my reason to exist.

We moved in together eventually. I pushed back. I was scared. I've always been hesitant to make big life decisions but in hindsight we should have done it sooner. What in the world was there to worry about? We spent every waking second together as it was. I had the same anxiety about getting engaged and having a baby. Maybe that's just how I'm built. Something inside me puts up a wall. The great thing about Clare is she knows exactly how to break it down.

When it comes to my career, Clare has been my biggest supporter by far. When no one believed in me, she did. Not only that, she encouraged me to start making videos, without which who knows where I would be today. I certainly wouldn't be writing this book from my ivory tower looking down on you peasants.

Before every show, she sits me down and allays my fears. When she says that I'm going to be great I really believe her, because when it comes to comedy or videos or anything to do with work, she tells me if something is shit.

We have travelled the world together and shared experiences most people only dream of. From packed theatres in Australia to clubs in New York, we have seen and done so much through comedy; all of which I owe to her. We may seem very outgoing but, sorry to break that illusion, we are old people at heart. We honestly prefer to be at home. Apart from cosy crime and cups of tea, we especially love the sunsets we can see from our house. I remember sitting on a beach in Hawaii watching a world-famous sunset and we both said almost at the same time, "Our sunsets are better." We have no interest in going clubbing or being a part of that fake Instagram/internet personality lifestyle. We would much rather be tending to our garden, which is hilarious when you consider what a lot of people probably think this loudmouth offensive comedian is like.

On the 23rd of July 2022, we got married. It was a beautiful day with all our family and friends. Clare looked absolutely amazing. Her dress was phenomenal and she looked like a princess. Her make-up, her hair, everything was perfect. It may sound strange but since I was a kid I really did dream of a wedding like this. While planning — and what a pain in the arse planning a wedding is — Clare made it very clear that she didn't want a big wedding; she wanted to elope. But, being the bridezilla I am, I talked her into having one. She was very nervous in the lead-up. For months she was fretting about walking down the aisle. In the end, however, it was me who spent the whole day freaking out while she remained calm and relaxed. In the end, Clare was right; we should have eloped. Why spend $140 a head on people you barely know and will probably never see again? That's the killer with a wedding, regardless of how many times you vow that you will not have strangers at your wedding eating your food and drinking your beer, at some point walking down the aisle you ask yourself, *who the fuck is that guy?*

We decided to exchange vows in private and I cried like a toddler who's had his blocks taken away. I wept, I sniffled, and I couldn't even look at her. I was an absolute mess. That day just meant so much to both of us. Finally, it had all come together. We were husband and wife. I felt whole and so very happy.

So why am I telling you all this? For one, it gets me in the good books with my dear wife. But none of this would have happened if I hadn't made all those mistakes early on. If I hadn't dated the nut jobs. If I hadn't gotten my heart broken as a young buck. I'm positive if I missed out on any one of those experiences then I wouldn't have met Clare. I actually had to be talked into going out that night I spotted her outside McDonald's, and thank god I did. So don't allow all those experiences to pass you by. Take them on board, learn from them, and enjoy them, because one day you'll look back and laugh at the dumb shit you once did. Or you could decide not to heed any of my warnings in this chapter, date someone just based on shit that doesn't matter, choose *not* to notice the signs that this person is not the one for you, they are not your best friend and you are not in this for the right reasons. That is up to you.

But I hope you go out and have fun and make dumb decisions — but don't sign a contract to spend the rest of your life with them. What the fuck is wrong with you? Just know that there really is a perfect relationship out there. There is someone who will keep you the happiest you have ever been right up until your final breath. Yes, they're hard to find. And yes, you'll have to work on yourself. But guess what? Everything worthwhile in life takes work. Do not settle until you are sure they are the one for you. And always marry your best friend.

Chapter 9: **Free speech**

YOU MAY never have given this much thought, but your right to speak freely is so valuable that people throughout history have fought and died just so you can keep doing it. The freedom to think, question, offend and speak *must* be held sacred. It *must* be protected. In this chapter, I want you to consider the threats to your own mind. I want you to understand how important it is to fight for your freedom of speech. I want you to understand that it's as important as the oxygen you breathe.

Right now it seems like we have travelled back in time. The way we are cornered into thinking and speaking in certain ways borders on the autocratic. Domineering new cult-like thought processes have infected large factions of modern society and, a bit like black mould, it's hidden in plain sight and spreads rapidly without intervention.

This is not new, it's happened before . . . Ever since the evolution of speech, people have tried to control it. Freedom of expression is as deadly to those in power as a gash in the hull of a ship is to its buoyancy. Those who rule with an iron fist have always policed it. Kings and queens, emperors and popes destroyed anyone who dared to question their leadership or right to rule. More people than you can imagine have been killed for speaking their minds throughout history. Since its inception, religion controlled people and their will with threats of the big man upstairs smiting the ever-living shit out of you if you dared question the church's beliefs or teachings. This is, and was a marvellous way to control large groups of people; it might very well be the ultimate way.

Free speech is a common denominator in the best countries in the world; this is perhaps why so many countries have laws protecting it. The US has it written into its constitution in the first amendment. England's *Human Rights Act* 1998 states that "Everyone has the right to freedom of expression" (except during a coronation).

Then we come to Australia, which has nothing. In fact, "The Australian Constitution does not explicitly protect freedom of expression."[3]

Well, that's fucked. In Australia, the only people who have protected speech are politicians speaking in Parliament, in the form of something known as "parliamentary privilege". The English brought this over with them in the 18th century.

---

3   humanrights.gov.au/our-work/rights-and-freedoms/freedom-information-opinion-and-expression

So the pollies are protected, but what about everyone else? We're royally fucked. That's the technical term for it, by the way.

The fight for free speech dates back to ancient Greeks. Somewhere around 400 BCE the ancient Athenians decreed that open debate and tolerance of negative opinions of authority was a necessary part of a high-functioning society. What an interesting thought. The guys throwing gold medals to blokes wrestling in the nude had more protections than most modern Australians. But it makes sense. How could all these free-thinking people, the philosophers and the stoics, have existed and had such an impact on the thousands of years that followed without the ability to think and speak without constraint?

The truth is, when speech is controlled, so to is thought. And just like our thoughts, our words sometimes spill out, and this is where new ideas come from. Regrettably, not all ideas that are spewed forth are fully thought-out or respectful — they may even be offensive — but we must be willing to accept bad ideas as *unfinished* ideas otherwise we risk never allowing the great ones to see the light of day.

If freedom of speech was being defended by the great thinkers of ancient Greece the polar opposite happened in Nazi Germany. The Nazi party, via Joseph Goebbels who was in charge of propaganda, enforced strict controls over all forms of expression. The punishment if you stepped out of line was a one-way ticket to one of the regime's many camps, if not death. Newspapers, radio, books, *everything* was controlled. Book burning literally took place. Libraries were stormed and anything that was anti-Nazi, or pro-Communist or Jewish was destroyed. Hitler and the leaders of the Nazi party saw free speech as a threat to their power and authority, and they committed genocide to keep control.

You would think we would have learnt from history but it appears we haven't. We are doing our own book burning when we change "offensive" texts such as Roald Dahl's work to remove mean words like "ugly" or "fat". Sure, this isn't as extreme as the Nazi party's mindset, no one is saying that, but it is a very slippery slope. The inclusivity police are hell-bent on seeking absolute power.

George Orwell's novel *1984* is famous for depicting a world without freedoms, where expression, thought and speech are all strictly controlled. Big Brother is always watching, listening and enforcing the laws of the new dystopian land. 2 + 2 = 5 is blatant propaganda; it's a lie! But you *must* believe it and if you dare speak up or correct that equation your life as you know it is over. We all know 2 + 2 = 5 is wrong, but it's a fallacy that is taught and enforced as fact in *1984*. You can make comparisons to our world with equations like this. When beliefs and fake truths are forced on people for long enough, a new generation, who doesn't know better, accepts it as unquestionable truth.

Here's an example: men can have babies.

This statement is obviously incorrect but ask around and you'll find plenty of people who think that it's true. I once said in a video that obviously men can't have babies. Well, a friend got in touch and angrily explained that I was so wrong and so hurtful. Most hilariously (and terrifyingly) of all, she said, "The science is changing". No, the science is not changing, you have just been indoctrinated into a world where propaganda is truth and the actual truth is hate speech. I'm not saying men can't be fathers or dads to children they didn't birth. Of course they can, but *biologically* and *logically* they cannot bear children.

This is what happens when totalitarianism takes over. Throughout history, whenever populations are subjected to absolute control and oppression, freedom of speech is the first thing that's taken away. We saw this just recently during the COVID-19 pandemic. Anything that went against the mainstream narrative was deemed "misinformation" and was suppressed. Anyone expressing these opinions was banned from social media. Anyone planning rallies off the back of that information was questioned by police, if not charged. Yes, some people were peddling crackpot theories, and yes, there was plenty of genuine misinformation flying about, but some of these ideas and beliefs, which were being brought to light by doctors risking their medical licences, have now been confirmed as actual facts. This was science that was not only being ignored, it was basically banned.

This has left the establishment and governments all over the world ruling over populations who don't trust them in the slightest, which I think is a good thing.

—

Just as religion has always controlled the masses with the threat of the charge of blasphemy, we have new religions doing this now, condemning free speech as hatred. In fact, they believe speaking freely could very well be the worst thing you can do. Many see offence, the by-product of people speaking freely, as equal to violence. I hear and read about how words are considered as violence in many woke circles. Allow me to spell this out: words are *not* violence. They are *never* violence. We are taught this from a very young age with the adage "sticks and stones . . .". This may be an unpopular opinion and I may shock you all with this next statement, but are you ready? Words *cannot hurt* you, dickhead.

But these new religions will have you believe exactly the opposite, that people must be protected from certain sounds we make with our mouths; that certain human beings cannot deal with these words, but some can, and the ones who can't must be saved by everyone else because they are too weak to hear those words. Could you imagine anything more offensive than that?

—

Since the 2010s, young people in Western societies have had to deal with rules that apply to speech. We all have guidelines we try to abide by, such as, be kind to people and don't say horrible things. For example, you or I would not walk up to a fat couple on the street and say, "G'day, you fat fucks." You just wouldn't. That is a social norm. You may think, *If there is freedom of speech maybe you should be able to do that if you want to.* Well, yes you *should* be able to say whatever you like and most of the time you *can* say anything to anyone. There are no laws against it, you won't get locked up, you will just seem like a crazy arsehole and this is the reason we don't do it. However, there *are* some restrictions on what we can and cannot say in public (which includes the internet). If you transgress, you can be punished, even if you are speaking the truth. You might lose your job, your status, or maybe even visitation rights to your children.

Take a look at Scotland. It sounds ridiculous but Scotland has one of the most authoritarian governments in the Western world. Over the past few years their government has been working on a piece of legislation called the *Hate Crime and Public Order Bill*. Straight off the bat with that title everyone thinks to themselves, *Sure, I'll get behind that, hate crimes are terrible*. That's what any logical human being would think. Once you start to read the Bill however you start to worry, particularly because there are parts of it that are completely undefined. Here's an example.

Section 3 — Offences of stirring up hatred

> In section 3 of the Bill, it states that it is an offence to stir up hatred against different races, ages, disabilities, social or cultural groups (vegans?), religion, sexual orientation, transgender identity and variations in sex characteristics (whatever that means).

Now, I'm not suggesting anyone in those groups should be subjected to hatred, but what in the fuck does "stirring up" hatred mean? That is what is known as a very fucking grey area and it could be abused by whoever wants to. Potentially you could go to jail, actually be locked up, because you said, "Gay people shouldn't be allowed to marry." You could argue that is stirring up hatred against the LGBTQI+ community. It's ridiculous that people think gay people shouldn't be allowed to marry but if you *do* think it, you should be allowed to say it; that is free speech.

At this point you may be going, *Okay, if you have opinions just keep them to yourself and you won't get in trouble.* Firstly, shut the fuck up. Secondly, if you said something that could "stir up hatred" in your own home, at your dinner table, and someone in your family wanted to run to the police or someone walking by the house heard it and wanted to dob you in, they could. You can be locked up for speaking your mind in your own fucking home! You can even go to jail for possessing offensive material. If I was in Scotland and made a video critical of the Catholic church and you downloaded it, you can be locked up because I'm "stirring up hatred" against a religion and you're complicit. It's not child porn for fucksake (speaking of the Catholic church), it's just words!

The Bill passed on 11 March 2021, with 82 votes in favour, 32 votes against, and 4 abstentions.

—

One great Scotsman faced the brunt of the Scottish legal system well before the Bill was drafted. His name is Mark Meecham (sounds like I'm in fight club) but he's more commonly known as Count Dankula. *Forbes* described Count Dankula as a "low-level comedian" who "on YouTube taught his girlfriend's pug Buddha to raise its paw in a Nazi salute". Pretty great publicity for a "low-level comedian" to bag an article in *Forbes*. In Australia, low-level comedians only get radio shows no one listens too and guest roles on TV shows everyone hates; so old Dank is outdoing them all.

In 2016 Count Dankula uploaded a video which was viewed 3 million times. In the video he disgustingly made his girlfriend's pug dog do Nazi salutes, and told the dog to "gas the Jews" and other vulgar and offensive things. Now was Dank doing this to hurt Jewish people? No, he wanted to take an adorable animal and see if his girlfriend would still find it adorable if it did something abhorrent. That's the joke — it's a juxtaposition between atrocity and cute little puggsy wuggsy. So what happens as a result of this obvious and funny joke? And if you say it's not funny, shut up, no one cares. I laughed, others laughed, therefore it's funny. Well, Count Dankula was arrested and locked in a cage under the *Communications Act* of 2003. He was released shortly after but that's not the point. He was arrested for *a joke* and two years later he was charged with breaching the law. The court said Dank's claim that the video was for his girlfriend and that it was designed to make her laugh "lacked credibility" because Dank's girlfriend didn't subscribe to his YouTube channel (how rude of her). What the fuck is that shit, Scotland.

The outcome, after much public backlash, was this: no prison time but Dank was fined 800 pounds (about $2000 bucks AUD). Dank refused to pay so a year later the government just took it from his bank account. Does that not terrify anyone else? A government, reacting this outrageously to something which is so obviously a joke, were so hell-bent on controlling this man's speech, they locked him in a cage and took his money — all under the guise of protecting minorities.

Count Dankula and the people of Scotland are not alone. Canadians have their own fight for freedom under their power-loving government. Dr Jordan Peterson was a professor at a Canadian university when he infamously said he would not be forced by law to call students by their chosen pronouns. He said he would happily do so if asked by a student, but if he were compelled by law under the threat of a fine, job loss or, in the most extreme, jail time, he would refuse on the basis of free speech being worth fighting for. This all came after the Canadian government made a change to their human rights act and the criminal code to include offences against gender identity and gender expression on the list of prohibited behaviour. Which could mean that if you refer to me with the wrong pronoun, you just broke the law.

The Canadian truckers who protested the vaccine mandates which allowed them to cross borders and continue working received a lot of negative press all around the world. It seemed like a coordinated attack. What left many people with a very bitter taste in their mouths was the distinct lack of action against other protests that occurred in the same period. It went further because these truckers and their supporters held views seen to be dangerous by the all-powerful Canadian Prime Minister Justin "Son of Castro" Trudeau (look up the Castro thing, no idea if it's true, Snopes.com says it's false, but it's funny). Trudeau came out and tweeted, seemingly out of nowhere, "Today in the House, Members of Parliament unanimously condemned the antisemitism, Islamophobia, anti-Black racism, homophobia, and transphobia that we've seen on display in Ottawa over the past number of days. Together, let's keep working to make Canada more inclusive." It was pretty funny stuff coming from a bloke who loves a bit of blackface. Trudeau's declaration was not only unwarranted, it was surely done to take any credibility away from the protesters and their freedom of speech. Then in another attempt to control people speaking freely, the Canadian government froze the bank accounts of those involved in the protest, an action that if taken in any other circumstances would be seen as an unforgivable act of tyranny.

In this modern world, we no longer threaten people with the power of the almighty, or the damnation of hell, or label them as a witch if they speak against the church or whoever is in power. Now we call them a bigot, a racist or transphobic, Islamophobic or homophobic. Free thinkers won't have god knocking on their door, but they may have their boss, or maybe the giants of social media, banishing them. This can happen to anyone. If you lose your Facebook account or YouTube page, it may not lose you any sleep but for some of us, not to sound like a dickhead here, it's how we speak to the world. Losing access to that just for saying what we believe to be real and true (and often is), is simply Orwellian.

There are now vast swathes of populated areas — more often than not in the big cities — where free speech is considered hate speech and, allegedly, anyone who speaks freely does so only to do damage. Those who think this way have been indoctrinated into their new chosen religion, be that feminism, the fat positivity movement or trans rights. Whatever the cause, the rules that govern these religious cults are not to be broken and god help you if they are. Based on everything we have learnt over the past decade or more, the question now is who is more important: those speaking their mind and their freedom of speech or those who may be offended?

That then begs the question: am I a free speech absolutist? I think I have to be, for believing in free speech while restricting some kinds of speech is oxymoronic. There are many things I think you shouldn't say. I don't think you should say that you believe the holocaust never happened but I will defend your right to do so. Do I agree with everything Donald Trump has ever said? No — but I will defend his right to say it. Hateful speech does exist, but we must allow it, it must be protected, and we must grant people the freedom to use it if they see fit. Some of you may feel it must be stopped. If that is you, then you may use your free speech to defeat what you deem hateful and this is done . . . ready for it? . . . *through speech*. Bad ideas are defeated by great ideas.

We must not allow Facebook, Instagram or pre-Musk Twitter (or post) to be the arbiters of what is deemed hate speech and what is not because that follows a very clear path of destruction. It ends with them becoming the adjudicators of truth or, as in *1984*, the Ministry of Truth.

Hate speech should be controlled by the people, not the government or big corporations. It's nothing short of a recipe for disaster. It shocks me how many young people subscribe to the concept that what is deemed hate speech, misinformation or anything that runs against the mainstream narrative should be dictated by a vocal minority. This goes against everything it is to be young! We must challenge authority, fight against the establishment and demand our freedoms.

Being offended means nothing. To quote the great Australian comedian Steve Hughes, "So what? Be offended. Nothing happens!" And it is because of this very obvious fact of offence not causing spontaneous combustion that no one should be protected from being offended. Not one human being deserves to be protected in this manner, at least not under the threat of the law or government intervention. If you walk up to a pregnant woman and say, "You look mighty fat today", you might cop a slap across the face and may very well deserve it. There may be consequences, you can't just run around being a piece of shit all day and not receive some feedback (although some would argue I, and many other comedians, have made careers by doing just that). But there is a difference between making a joke and being a horrible person. We have the ability to cause offence if we choose to. What matters is our *intent*.

When we question something or talk about someone who is protected from offence or debate, what happens? We are banned from that social media page, we might be deplatformed, we may lose friends, we might even lose our jobs. We are, in a modern way of looking at it, penalised for having the wrong opinion or being offensive. It can result in our lives being altered and then being forced into having the "right" opinion or not being offensive before being allowed to return. This isn't anything new and the wokerati need to realise by forcing people to do what they deem appropriate is exactly what the kings and queens, emperors and popes have sought to do throughout history.

For the longest time, anyone who questioned the church's authority was seen as greatly offensive. Speaking in a blasphemous manner would have seen you hanged until you were dead. Thomas Aikenhead, a Scottish student in the late 1600s, was 20 years old when he was arrested for saying crazy things like, "Theology was a rhapsody of ill-invented nonsense" and that he "preferred Muhammad to Christ". The prosecution demanded he receive the death penalty to set an example to others who might otherwise express similar opinions. He was hanged in January 1697.

The death penalty for atheism still exists in 13 countries today.

Thank god I'm not going to be killed for tweeting that "All Lives Matter" (which of course is very offensive as you must say "Black Lives Matter"), but I may lose all my worldly possessions, potential career opportunities and income. The people who control free speech may look different today but they are still very much the same.

—

Without people being offended by free speech many notions and customs may not be as common as they are today. Learning tolerance and how to take offence without losing your shit is a necessary part of growth.

Galileo was convicted in 1633 for daring to support

Copernicus in his outrageous hypothesis that the Earth revolved around the sun — the opposite to the widely held and indoctrinated beliefs of the time. He was locked up and his work destroyed for offending the establishment. Gay people offended everyone in the 20th century just by existing and demanding to be seen. Without that offence, they wouldn't be seen as a very normal part of today's society and rightfully so. The women's suffrage movement . . . Rosa Parks at the back of the bus . . . the English reformation . . . even the abolition of slavery. All of these actions were offensive to the powers that be and attempts were made to ban or stop them to create a safe space, to "save" everyone. The truth of the matter is that without offence, we do not move forward. The war against offence is the opposite of progression. A civilisation needs its people to think clearly and freely. Putting constraints on these very simple ideas does nothing but send us back to the Dark Ages, and that should terrify and motivate all of us.

Of course, I think about this more than most because I depend on free speech for an income. Sure, in some videos I may toe the line of what is seen to be appropriate, but in my stand-up I cross that line on a nightly basis and when I do, and those words said in jest hit the ears of someone who cannot deal with anything spoken for the purpose of a joke, these precious people act as if war has been declared and they must do absolutely everything in their power to stop it. They contact all of the like-minded acolytes in their vicinity, they demand action from them and like that first domino falling, the chain reaction is swift and explosive.

An 1859 essay called "On Liberty" by English philosopher

John Stuart Mill showed why freedom of speech, thought and expression are so necessary to basic human function. He penned what the intelligent among us have known throughout history to be true, yet was never demonstrated in literature. He argued that there were two sides, constantly competing against each other in a tug of war over truth: authority vs liberty. Authority was and is the government, it's the corporations and religions, but it's also the vocal minority, the ones who dictate the rules because they speak with the most vigour. To counter that, Mill wrote that the citizens must be the ones who control the government — they must protect their liberty. In the Western world this does occur, but in many circumstances, it's nothing more than an illusion.

Mill set out three basic liberties in order of importance to the individual and the majority:

- The freedom of thought and emotion: this is free speech, the thoughts we have which become the lexicon of ideas.
- The freedom to pursue tastes even if they are seen as "immoral" (unless they do harm).
- The freedom to unite, so long as the involved members are of age, the involved members are not forced, and no harm is done to others.

To break it down into one simple point from philosopher to comedian, as long as you're not hurting anyone or breaking the law, then go for it. The problem is, as we have seen in this chapter, the concept of pain through spoken word has grown like a disease and because of this concept, laws are being implemented to constrain our thoughts. As a consequence, following Mill's simple maxim is becoming more and more difficult.

Supressing ideas is dangerous and, please, heed this warning: we do not grow as a society or as individuals when we are told what we can and cannot say or what we can or cannot see or hear. Many great ideas that we now base our lives on were once regarded as offensive speech that had to be controlled. Fundamental ideas, concepts and attitudes would never have seen the light of day if not for someone daring to speak out freely.

Freedom of speech must be protected, saved and seen as sacred, for without it we are just trained apes mimicking the lives and beliefs of the other primates around us.

Chapter 10: Be careful of new religions

BE VERY careful of new religions, they are looking for someone just like you and they might not get you now, but in time, when you are at your weakest, they will pounce. We live in an opportune time for parasitic ideas, thoughts and doctrines to latch onto you. In many cases they never let go. For some, they bite down into your very personality and you *become* the parasite.

As we saw in the previous chapter, religion is a great way to control people. Perhaps that's why it has been a constant throughout the evolution of homo sapiens. Apart from control, it was invented by different groups across the globe to explain the unexplainable.

"Why does the sun set?"

"It is god's will."

"Who creates lightning?"

"Thor of course."

As humans evolved, we had no fucking idea what was going on so why not blame the gods? We all have them, even cultures separated by half a world. When you break it down, there's really only a handful of comparable beliefs spread across ancient human civilisations — and most feature dragons and pyramids. Read into that what you will. Based on absolutely zero study, when we created our gods, whoever they may be, that belief created the rules, laws and understanding of what we can and cannot do. Religion fits so perfectly into a human's life; we are all desperate for meaning and answers and for many millions of people, religion gives us just that. Unfortunately, it's probably bullshit. We all end up in a hole in the ground (or as a nice ash fertiliser) with the lights off forever. Then again, maybe we don't. Who the fuck knows.

Anyway, over time and with the help of science we learnt that no, it wasn't any one god who controlled the sun. In fact, god had nothing to do with creating the earth. It turns out we aren't even the centre of the universe. The universe is so expansive our feeble minds cannot even comprehend how big it is. To understand infinite size like that you would have to be infinitely wise, like a god perhaps?

We have for the most part — at least in the West (except for parts of America) — moved away from religion. I became an atheist at a very young age, but as I got older and came to appreciate the great unknowns of the universe, I began to understand that saying there is no god or creator is just as foolish as saying "my god is the right god". The truth is, you just don't know.

As we've lost our attachment to religion we've lost a part of us, which we now must fill will something else, something that acts like a religion, something to live by, believe in and, when it comes down to it, be fearful of. You may be quite surprised at some of the new religions on my list because they are everywhere. Perhaps you have never considered them as "religions" at all.

Veganism is the first that springs to mind. If you are unfamiliar with my YouTube channel you may not know this but I do take issue with vegans quite a bit. I've even turned it into a profitable business selling "Fuck Vegans" beef jerky. Like a religious fundamentalist, you will not change a vegan's mind. They have been indoctrinated into a way of thinking and arguing. Much like Muslims go to the mosque, vegans head down YouTube rabbit holes, surround themselves with like-minded individuals and soon find themselves in an impregnable echo chamber. The vegan world is comparable to the inner workings of a religious sect; they are told what to believe, provided evidence as to those beliefs and more importantly told how to defend them. Transgenderism is also a religion. Spend five minutes on pre-Musk Twitter and you'll find out how fanatical they are.

What makes a good religion? Beliefs and submission to the teachings. Religion dares you to forget your ability to think rationally. All you are left with are the rules and thoughts of others within that cult. Sorry, religion.

For example, Adam and Eve spoke to a snake and then ate

an apple, now everyone has to die for "original sin". People who practise the teachings of the Bible believe that god put two people in the Garden of Eden and spoke to a talking snake.

Okay . . . replace that with:

Gender is fluid.

Women are just as strong as men.

Babies don't know their gender.

Children should receive hormone blockers.

And you're a bigot if you don't want to fuck a trans person.

You may not be a part of the group, the cult, the religion, unless you take these on as your mantra.

The next step is controlling the speech of others and those around you. Demanding we all speak in a certain fashion is integral to these religions taking over and dominating people. Without control of speech and thought, these religions have no power.

Both vegans and the trans community have their own version of the devil, the evil entity who's coming to take everything perfect in the world. The religious have the devil from hell, the vegans have the carnivores (or me) and the trans community has anyone who thinks men can't have babies. The problem with all of this, of course, is that being welded to our ideas destroys the potential for us to develop into better versions of ourselves. What happens next is that the people I'm talking about here aren't just tied to their ideas — they have become them.

The same can be said for political leanings. In the US you are either a Republican or a bitch, a Democrat or a bigot.

In the same way religion recruits children through families, political parties also go after the young and impressionable. Many voters do not vote with their heads, they vote as their parents vote. In the US, the tension between Blue and Red is comparable to Israel and Palestine, minus the rockets of course. These people, on one side who consider themselves right wing and the other who are proudly left wing, will go as far as to dedicate their lives to powerful multimillionaires looking to run the world. Sounds like a certain religion based in somewhere near Rome now, doesn't it?

With the decline in religion across the Western world, we are seeing an enormous uptick in individuals looking for meaning, desperate for structure. But that's not necessarily a good thing, especially when it's built on a lie. We are gullible creatures, desperate to belong, and by finding yourself in one of these houses of worship you may find the course of your life changes instantly and eternally. But don't be sucked in. Be as sceptical about religions as you are about their replacements.

Chapter 11: **You are weak**

THERE IS a trap set for us humans; a prison that attracts those who seek the easiest passage through life. The trap acts like a big hug, telling you it's all going to be all right. It helps you deal with all the problems you face by pushing the blame onto others. Sure, sometimes a cuddle from the universe is beneficial, it may even be necessary, but should you rely on it? Should you demand it? Should you go through life pursuing it? No, no, no!

I'm talking of course about the path of least resistance. I've mentioned it a few times already in this book. It's a disease in which weakness flourishes, pity is desired and dreams never become reality. At some point in the last few decades we have not begun encouraging weakness, we've started *expecting* it. Men and women, the young and the old, are all doing it. Worse, they don't see it as something shameful, but rather something that should be celebrated and recognised as a great triumph.

I'm not talking about men crying, or women being emotional. Past generations would have seen this as weakness, but these days we recognise it's a regular part of human expression, regardless of your gender. With men it's actually now encouraged, which I think is a good thing. Expressing emotions or being emotional, caring or loving is part of being a well-rounded human. As long as you're not breaking down in tears constantly then there is nothing wrong with it at all.

No, I'm talking of actual weakness, hiding when you encounter adversity, cowering from fear and even life itself, being selfish, and lying to save yourself. There is one popular cult where this is so prevalent it is expected of all people who look similar to those in the cult. I'm talking about the cult of "body positivity" and it goes by many names:

- Fat positivity movement
- Healthy at every size
- Body acceptance movement
- Body neutrality
- Fat Lives Matter

I may have made that last one up, though you can imagine it sitting in someone's Twitter bio next to their blue tick. All of these movements have some beneficial elements. Body positivity by definition is rooted in promoting self-confidence and being happy with what you have. You may have an arm or a few teeth missing, acne scars, or growths — none of this should make you feel inferior. I had terrible varicose veins in my legs from about age 15 to 27 years old. They were ugly and I was ashamed of them. If I was in a proper body-positive mindset I would have looked at them and said, "These make me, me. I'm proud of them." All lies but it would have made me feel better.

The actual body positivity movement, which has turned into the fat positivity movement, isn't concerned with those ailments or issues we are born with at all, it's concerned with being obese, staying obese and encouraging others to remain obese by demanding inaction. Even board-certified doctors are weighing in (great pun) on this trend. Natasha Larmie, who calls herself "the fat doctor", decided to do the rounds of breakfast TV in the UK in 2021 making statements like going on a diet "is the greatest predictor of weight gain". Some of her other classics included:

> "Every body is a good body."
> "Weight loss is actually not good for our health."
> "The weight loss industry will try to convince you I'm wrong."
> "Health is a privilege you are born into."

Just utter shit, this was broadcast at a time when the world was either still locked down or coming out of lockdown due to COVID-19. And can you guess the biggest predictor of death due to COVID? Of almost 1,000,000 people hospitalised in the US in the early part of the pandemic, "most of the hospitalized patients had underlying conditions". By "underlying conditions", we're primarily talking about diabetes, hypertension and heart failure — which are primarily caused by being overweight. We shut down the world for COVID-19, killed businesses, broke the hearts of billions and still carried on promoting one of the main contributing factors to your chance of survival. Obesity was cherished by some, promoted by others and forcefully celebrated by all. Another contributing factor to COVID mortality was being elderly. Don't you think if people could mitigate that risk they would have? If you could somehow reverse ageing and that would help you not die, you would do it.

It is ridiculous and dangerous to live the lifestyle promoted by the body-positive society. You may not think people are actually out there promoting obesity. Well, I dare you to spend five minutes on fat acceptance Instagram; you'll change your tune in an instant. You'll see thousands of Instagrammers explaining that you don't have to be fit to be beautiful, that you don't have to be thin to be accepted and that's all fine, I agree, but what ruins it is what they then go on to proudly proclaim, stuff like, "I'm brave for wearing a bikini when I weigh 200 kilograms" or "What I eat in a day as a fat person not trying to lose weight".

Sure, you can have these thoughts about yourself. Be as insane as you want. But what makes all of this grotesque — and extremely dangerous — is that these people demand everyone else agrees with them. They expect that you lie to yourself and request that if you are a fat person you follow suit. Dare to question this mindset and you will be punished with a good helping of cancellation due to fatphobia. Because it's fatphobic to say being fat is not healthy. How mad is that?

Search the hashtag #FatPositive on TikTok and you will see a never-ending collection of extremely obese women explaining why they won't bow to society's expectations and become smaller or eat less. These social media sirens lure people in with each video, going into great detail about how it's normal to be obese and you *must not change*. They aren't bad people; they, like all of us, are just trying to find their place in the world. Their lives are difficult and at some point they discovered someone on TikTok or Instagram who allowed them out of the shackles that was the hatred they had for themselves. Now that's not inherently bad, but when it becomes detrimental to your health then someone must put a stop to it. When it's encouraging a generation of young and impressionable minds to give up, we must do something.

Would we step in if someone was encouraging others to smoke, or drive drunk? We have laws designed to stop people from smoking, because it kills people, and the same can be said for drunk and drug driving. Yet we have influencers promoting a lifestyle of obesity which last year was right up there with smoking when it comes to the top five causes of death in Australia. That's why I'm passionate about this topic. That's why I've made jokes about it on stage, videos about it on YouTube and that's why I'm writing about it now. We have a sick population and bullshit fat propaganda is only making it worse.

—

Whenever I raise this issue, I am immediately met with, "Well, you hate fat people." No, I don't hate fat people at all. I just don't agree with the message that some weak people — who also happen to be fat — are spreading. It's a poor message designed for those in society who are predisposed to succumb to their natural tendencies — to follow the path of least resistance. It's a message tailor-made for those who listen to their own weakness and are easily trapped by the sweet songs of these body-positive sirens.

What's more, is it just me, or are the loudest and most prolific pro-fat propagandists always female? The representation of men in these body-positive circles (pun) is slim (pun) to none. Is it because men aren't fat? Obviously not, fat men are everywhere. Some 70 per cent of Australian men are overweight compared to around 56 per cent of Australian women. So why aren't blokes behaving like this?

I think I have the answer. Fat men are more honest with each other and themselves. If one of their favourite Instagram influencers looks at them through their iPhone covered in cracks and Doritos' dust and tells them that "being fat is beautiful" and "being fat is healthy", they will scoff and tell them to get fucked. They know it's a complete joke, nothing more than a lie to make themselves feel better about eating too much, not exercising enough and not caring about their health. If they do happen to buy into it, their mates will sit them down, laugh in their face and tell them to shut the fuck up. Some may see this as toxic masculinity, but I see it as nothing short of extreme accuracy.

There's another reason why I feel so passionately about

how bad the body positivity movement can be, and how dangerous the modern messaging is. It's pretty simple: when I was younger I was overweight. I can tell you from personal experience that being a fat kid absolutely sucks. It's one of the worst things that you can go through as a teenager. Trying to navigate the strange world you find yourself in at that age is hard enough. Being fat makes it so much harder. Just for starters, you have fuck all chance of getting a girlfriend, let alone sex. You find yourself behind in anything physical and you are the prime target for bullying.

But I didn't start off fat. Up until I was about 10 years old I was a very slim, fit-looking kid. I spent every afternoon riding my bike and playing with my mates. We did so many great things that involved being active, and some not so great things, like rock fights (yes, we used to throw rocks at each other from across a playground . . . if people think there is no difference between young boys and girls, you're being ridiculous).

But around the time I turned 10, my parents got Foxtel (cable TV). It was a fucking revelation. Naturally, I stopped going outside as much. I was obsessed, and watching the wrestling was my favourite pastime — this was the golden era of The Rock, Stone Cold and The Undertaker, so how could I resist. Combine my love of Foxtel with Pokémon on the Gameboy, PS1 and a diet high in snacks, the expansion of young Isaac Butterfield began. In the last two years of primary school I became borderline obese. I was bullied and this carried on into high school. I was "the fat kid" and I did try to change . . . but I always ended up taking the path of least resistance. I began diets but never stuck to them. I went running but never persevered. I went to the gym, but not enough. I played football and trained but ate a shit load of food . . .

Sure, I was weak. But the other problem was I knew nothing about nutrition. Back then, kids weren't told about calories in and calories out; we were just told to eat "healthily". For most kids, that really doesn't mean much. I was made to be overweight. My body was designed to be fat. I had (and still have) childbearing hips where fat loves to hang out. I was just lucky I'm six foot eight so there was a big frame to hang all the weight off. In my final year of school, my football coach had a hard-on for cardio. We ran for hours and I was the fittest I had ever been. I was probably about 115 kilograms at that point.

After school not much changed, I was relatively fit and I could play football for almost a full game without being substituted. But I never *looked* overly fit. Every young man wants to look ripped and that's not the fault of society or bodybuilders even though their aesthetics are unachievable without steroids. Wanting to look fit, to be strong — or at least try — is built into our DNA. It is the ideal way to appear as a man. Why? Simple: it's fucking hard and it takes dedication, sacrifice and belief. Anything that is hard will attract two types of people: those who really want it and those who avoid it because they spend their entire lives desperately searching for the path of least resistance.

I spent my early twenties overweight, not huge but not ideal, and year after year I got just that little bit bigger. I guarantee you that if I didn't fix my lifestyle, my diet, my exercise routine — everything — I would now be morbidly obese. It took until I hit 134 kilograms (almost 295 pounds or 21 stone) before I made a major change. This change wasn't just based on weight, it was also due to the myriad other benefits I'd started investigating. I was about 24 years old when I discovered the ketogenic diet. I first heard about it on *The Joe Rogan Experience* podcast when he interviewed an author by the name of Gary Taubes. In his book *The Case Against Sugar*, Taubes explains how, like Big Tobacco, the sugar industry (yes, there is one of those) spent millions of dollars twisting the arms of scientists to put the blame of ill health squarely on the shoulders of fat and not sugar. It was a crock of shit. Study upon study have since shown that fats aren't the enemy we always thought them to be, and that sugar is the real culprit. This all leads us to the keto diet, a high-fat, low-carb diet, rich in meats and low in grains, rice and potatoes. What really excited me was the fact that this diet had been used in the past to treat young children with medication-resistant epilepsy. Combine that with the idea of keto helping you lose weight and I was in.

Over the next two months (and don't start this without checking with your doctor, just because I love it doesn't mean your doctor will) I went from a diet high in carbohydrates and sugars to one high in fat.[4] I cut out everything I loved: all sweet things, fruit, ice cream; and anything savoury that

---

4 But do check with your doctor before changing to a new diet.

was hiding loads of carbs, like chips, chicken schnittys, pasta and pizza.

It was hard at first, but after a few weeks I started to notice changes. Two kilos down, then four, then eight, then 10. Holy shit, suddenly I was 20 kilograms lighter! I barely had one day off for over 12 months. At the end of the diet I weighed 94 kilograms (207 pounds or 14.8 stone). It was a massive loss. I was a completely different person. I felt great. I retired from football at this point and was in the gym every day loving it. I went back to pre-season training and I could run; I was in front of everyone. For 15 years I was at the back of the pack but here I was, leading the team. It was an unbelievable feeling. All I needed to do was gather knowledge, commit and sacrifice. And that's exactly what I did.

But then, I did something no one on a diet should do: I went on the road for my first Australian stand-up comedy tour, then followed it up with my first tour to the UK. This was over a period of two years and I put around 10 kilograms back on, but that also made sense. I'd fallen back into my old eating habits. When Natasha Larmie talks about diets never working this is what she means. People finish the diet and then start to put on weight again, but there is a way to deal with that. You have to realise it's not the diet's fault but yours. You were eating shit before, and when you start eating shit again, what the fuck did you think was going to happen?

I did not want to put on any more weight, so I hit the gym again, six days a week, in fact. I followed a training program that I developed after watching hundreds of hours of gym and workout content on YouTube (the program is available at the back of the book). But it all came to a grinding halt when COVID-19 arrived. Gyms, which were one of the only things people could do to remain healthy, were closed, so I decided to do something that I had always been terrible at and absolutely hated: I started running.

My goal and I promise you, you can do this as well, was to run 10 kilometres (6 miles). For me this was a massive undertaking, but I started small and I didn't start with distances. I started with running for certain amounts of time and this is where I think people either succeed or are defeated by the evil thoughts you experience when running. On day 1, I laced up my shoes, I had my timer on my phone and I ran a grand total of five whole minutes. I repeated that three other days that week. I knew that if I was going to hit that 10 kilometre mark, it was going to take time. The week after I upped it to 15 minutes, then the week after to 20, then all the way up to 30. At this point I was running three days per week and hitting distances of 5 kilometres, meaning I was on track to run 10 kilometres in under an hour.

I found very early on regardless of whether you are running 1 kilometre or 50, your brain will try and get you to quit almost immediately. You are weak, never forget that. The only reason we get things done is because we push our brain and inner monologue out of the way and tell it to get fucked. The only other tip I have for running, other than programming how long you will run for, is what you listen to. Many people listen to gym-like music, maybe a bit of metal like Simple Plan. Or, if you're a bit of a loose unit, some Nickelback. I listened to podcasts. Listening to podcasts keeps you at a steady pace. It also allows your mind to wander, you become part of the conversation, you learn, you listen and pretty soon you forget you are even running.

My times kept improving and after a few more weeks, the day arrived, I was going to run 10 kilometres, an entire hour of pavement pounding and — sorry for the lack of suspense — I fucking knocked it out of the park. I was extremely proud of myself. I've hated running my entire life. I was always last, I barely finished cross country at school and now I was doing 10 kilometres three days a week. One afternoon I decided to run a flat trail, rather than the hilly terrain I usually ran in. I managed to do the 10 kilometres in 49 minutes, which exceeded my expectations. After a while I fucked my knees up from running on the road, but when the going was good the butts got going.

The reason I'm telling you this is because while I was running — and also during every other important moment in my life — I had a nagging voice in my head telling me to give up. Instead of doing that, I fought tooth and nail to beat it. I can't imagine how hard it would have been to achieve what I did if I also had other voices, particularly from people I respected, telling me to give up, that I'm perfect just the way I am. Don't try harder, just accept yourself.

There are body-positive activists out there whose entire game is fighting the "evils" of normalising people going on a diet. They believe diet culture is built on the back of power structures like capitalism and the patriarchy, not to mention racism, proving something I've believed for quite some time: you can find a victim almost anywhere. They are turning the fight against obesity into a race war. In fact, whenever you see the term "anti-fatness" the term "anti-blackness" is not too far behind. If all of this is a shock to you, understand this: there's an entire subculture fighting for their rights as the world sees them, but it is not them who must change, it is *you*. We should all be eating less processed and more wholefoods, and a little bit less overall. If we do that for long enough we'll lose weight and therefore be less likely to die from illnesses associated with obesity.

Corporations are in on the fat-positivity movement, promoting people in bigger bodies (their term not mine), but I can guarantee you it's not out of the goodness of their hearts! In 2021, *Cosmopolitan* magazine famously included two overweight women on separate front covers with the caption "This is Healthy" printed below. They are not alone. Countless big businesses have seized the opportunity to advertise to the body-positivity community, from Dove to Bonds to JCPenney to Nike; and they are all pushing the message that health can be found at every size. There is nothing wrong with making clothes for bigger people. But think about why they are doing these campaigns that they are being celebrated for — they see an opportunity to take advantage of your desperate need to be accepted and they do everything they can to make you buy from them. Let me let you in on a little secret: if a company is telling you that all bodies are beautiful, that fat bodies are healthy and they follow it up with a call to action "Come and shop with us" they don't give a fuck about you. They aren't on your side, they just want your money.

As the movement has evolved, we have seen the rise of plus-sized models. In the beginning they were regular sizes, a size 12 here, maybe even a size 16. But along comes Tess Holliday. A giant woman, enormous, extremely obese, Tess throws on some lingerie, poses for a photo, posts it on Instagram and the comment section immediately fills up with:

"Yass queens!"

"You go, girl!"

"Flaunt it!"

Yet in reality, and I'm sorry in advance, she looks horrible. She is not a picture of health. She appears to be a very sick woman. If you are not familiar with her, google her. I'm not talking about a slightly overweight person here, I'm talking about someone who is morbidly obese. But she is someone whom obese women look up to because they believe they can still be beautiful and be that size. Maybe they can be beautiful at that size — beauty is in the eye of the beholder, after all — my point is she is an awful role model for big women because she isn't trying to help them lose weight and live longer, she is basically saying and doing nothing. As a consequence, her fans do nothing and over time they get bigger and bigger. Rather than addressing the problems they have when they are young or smaller, they are then forced to make a change when they are diagnosed with diabetes, or can't fall pregnant. Tess came out and said that she's recovering from an eating disorder and survived anorexia. Babe, saying you survived anorexia is like saying Hitler was a little peeved at the Jews. It's the understatement of the century. Yet despite all this, despite being huge, despite looking sick, the media have crowned her a beautiful inspiration.

While researching this chapter I came across endless websites that censor adjectives used to describe fat people. It's hilarious. They print the word Ob*sity instead of Obesity, or Ov*rweight not Overweight. It seems "large and in charge" humans are so delicate, not only must we change science to protect them, but the English language must also suffer the same fate. Can you imagine how deranged you must be to demand that? That's why I refer to ideologies like these as cult-like religions. They demand you leave any critical thinking at the door and make sure anyone who does question their philosophy is banished, never to return. There have been many debates over the years of pro-fat liberation (that's another one) arguing that the doctors and scientists have absolutely no idea what's going on and the fat army are correct because, well, they just feel like they are, this is all based on feelings. I'm not sure what the past decade has done to us as a collective, but it seems more than ever, everyone's feelings are paramount and matter above all else — even reality. Of course it's important to respect and be kind to others, but when that person argues without logic and relies on fallacies, how can you sit there and say nothing?

Yet that is exactly what most people do. They are so terrified of being labelled fatphobic and cancelled online that they will cower as if Godzilla waded up on shore (pun intended).

What I want you to take away from this chapter, is the understanding that if there is something you want to change about your body — maybe you are overweight, or maybe you are too skinny, perhaps you want to put on muscle, or run faster or further — you will encounter many people urging you to stop. They will tell you that you are fine the way you are. They will say you don't need to change for anyone else and all of that may very well be true. But only we know if changes must be made. Only we know if we are the best versions of ourselves and unless that person giving you advice to stay the same is in peak physical, mental and emotional health, then do *not* listen to them. Why would you listen to someone who hasn't done it themselves? You wouldn't ask a painter for advice on how to win at the stock market, so why ask someone who has given up on themselves on how you can be a better you?

If you are a fat kid, fat teen, fat adult male or female, I am living proof that you can change, that you can correct errors that have been with you since childhood and implement changes that will see you live a longer, happier and healthier life. I'm also living proof that this journey is life-long and a healthy diet and lifestyle aren't things you can just buy into for a few months or a year. They have to guide you for as long as you are on the planet. You will be better for it.

Whatever you do, do not fall into the traps set by those who secretly wish they were other versions of themselves, those who claim they'd give anything to change but instead try to corrupt the world around them by demanding others silence their rational minds, disregard science and lie to themselves in an attempt to find happiness. The truth for those people is that happiness will never be found. They may think they find it for a short period of time, because people are being nice to them, but that charade will quickly dissipate the moment it falls out of fashion with popular culture. We will have a generation who never implemented changes into their lives early enough and will unfortunately die at a younger age than they should. It is a very nice thing to say that "all bodies are beautiful" and health at every size is a gorgeous concept but unfortunately it is just not accurate. It's going to hurt more people than it helps in the long run.

In saying all that, lose some weight, you fat fucks. I did.

Chapter 12: **Mansplaining men**

THERE ARE countless books, articles, podcasts, events, apps and PDFs created by women, for women, to explain how hard it is to be a woman. The overriding theme is "If only men understood us it would all be easier". The target market for all this content however is not women; no, no no, it's the evil that walks the earth: *men*. If you want to feel awful about your gender feel free to check it all out. Everything is blamed on men. It becomes quite comical after a while. Pretend, just for a moment, that they are talking about anyone else other than men and you can just imagine the furious response — the absolute outrage.

But it got me thinking; if men make so many mistakes, then women probably make some as well, if not just as many. I know what a fucking sexist pig of a man I am. It must be the concentrated toxic masculinity on my face (beard). Maybe the word "mistake" is the wrong word. Maybe there are just some parts of masculinity and what it means to live life as a male that females can't quite grasp. Once again, how dare I suggest that women aren't brave, beautiful and entrepreneurial. If you suggested the complete opposite — that men are shit at understanding women — it would be met with a round of applause, a "Yass queen" and a ticker-tape parade, so fuck it.

Listen up, ladies, you are on notice.

Don't think this chapter is me attacking women. It's not. But believe me when I say: men don't understand you at all. This is thanks to the vast differences between the sexes, much to the dismay of many in these modern times. I'm sorry to say this, but men and women are *very different creatures*. Some may put this down to social engineering or "gender norms" but, for the most part, men and women are just plain different.

We are born differently. Don't get me wrong, some boys like playing with dolls and some girls with trucks but, on average, boys gravitate to trucks and girls to dolls. This is the case throughout the world and not just the Western world. It's exactly the same in countries where the "gender norms" are vastly different to ours and their populations aren't subjected to the influences that allegedly cause these "norms". Some parts of the world do not have access to TV, movies, or Instagram and yet the boys want to play with trucks and the girls with dolls. Why? It is built into our genetics to gravitate toward these activities and you may choose to take offence at that but no one gives a shit.

Now that we have established that it is very hard for men to understand women and we also know it's difficult for women to understand men, let's look at how we can improve the situation. Let's examine what makes us tick and what we don't like. This chapter is more for women if they want to understand what the fuck is going on in our heads, but it might also help you, as a man, realise you are not crazy. You are just like the rest of us, fucking insane.

Let me mansplain men to you.

We are lonely

What do men really want? You may think, cars, money or women. Well, sure, a lot of men believe they want those things, but they're not actually what we need. Plenty of happy men have none of those things. So do men *really* want?

Young men grow up to desire things that our society makes them believe they should. The same can be said for young women. As we grow older, we assume that these are the things that will make us happy so we still desperately seek them. Regrettably, more often than not, these things have no real value. They're superficial. The enjoyment we derive from these items regardless of the monetary value is often short-lived and does not alter the course of the person's life nor fulfil their dreams. You may one day buy a $200,000 car. It's great, to begin with, but soon enough it's just a car. Compare that to having a child or raising a dog; it's no competition. The car means nothing. So let's pull down this bullshit curtain of what it is to be a man, and what men want that was taught to us from generations past, and get down to some hard truths. More than anything else, men want three things: purpose, love and an outlet.[5]

Purpose

Without purpose we act like an engine, and eventually, we atrophy and die. This is why you see old men, let's say your grand- or great-grandfather, living a relatively healthy life while they're at work. But when they get to their mid-sixties, they retire, do nothing for a few years, and then they are fucking dead. They didn't just quit their jobs, they quit their reason to wake up every day. Your job should not be your reason for living but for many men in generations past their career was precisely that, their purpose. They may have started working when they were 14 years old and never missed a day of work. All of a sudden you expect them to just drop it all and pretend that everything's okay? No fucking way, it's impossible and the result is death. This is how serious purpose is in a man's life.

Young men can succumb to this as well. Say they leave school all excited, a year goes by, maybe two, and they wake up one day and ask, "What is the point of getting up and going to work another day? It means nothing to me. I hate the people there. Is life even worth living?" Momentum shifts and all of a sudden they are stuck, sinking deeper and deeper into the quicksand of despair.

---

5   I'm not saying women don't also need these things but this is about men.

Love
Men have to be loved, proper love. We want to find someone whom we somehow become a part of, experiencing the kind of love that almost hurts when you really think about it. When you find this person they can even become your purpose. That's the kind of love you want. Sure, it's risky because if they leave or the relationship breaks down, you lose love and purpose in one go. But I promise you it's worth that risk, because once you find that person, the one who will pick you up, listen to you and help solve your problems — and you will do the same for them — it makes life so much better on every level.

We are socially engineered to believe that love is something that only desperate damsels in distress need. Only the princess in the tower needs to be saved by love. The truth is that we, as men, don't realise how much we need love in our lives. Growing up we never really worry about it. We don't dream of our wedding day (although I did) or daydream of meeting our soulmate, or at least we would never admit it. This is a real shame because those of us who never find love never access the upgraded version of life and that's honestly too depressing to think about.

Many men are saved by meeting their partner and when we fall into a positive happy relationship it's like we are seeing colour for the first time. Everything is brighter, food tastes better, it's as if you can finally take a proper deep breath. This is why if it suddenly ends, we are broken, quietly navigating the very catacombs that are our minds, desperate for a way out.

Outlet

Men need an outlet. It can be almost anything. I refer to it as getting your "raas" out. Everyone builds stress up day to day and finding a way to deal with that is paramount. You could choose an unhealthy outlet, like smoking, drinking, drugs, cheating or jerking off until you're blue in the face. It may help short term but long term it just creates more problems that you will need to fix and therefore more stress to be dealt with later.

Alternatively, you could go to the gym, start boxing, or doing jiu-jitsu, and train the fucking house down. When I train I treat it like it is my job. I have to do it every day and I promise you, that kind of outlet is more powerful than alcohol or any anti-anxiety drugs. It grounds you and brings you back to earth. When you are stressed you become overwhelmed, then you panic and then you lose; but if you can find an outlet that brings your racing mind back to a speed that is manageable, all else seems insignificant and your anxiety and fear lose their voice. You can live again.

The problem for a lot of men is where the fuck to start. Particularly if you are in a job you hate. Well, firstly, there is always time to start again. I know you have a mortgage, student loans or some reason you think you can't make a change. You can but it just takes time. It takes sacrifice and dedication but you *can* make the change.

The mistake many white-collar men (and some women) make is that they think men who really hate their job are just working in a shitty office surrounded by dickheads. That is the case in some situations, obviously. But all of that changes when the job is doing something we call in Australia "hard yakka", or hard work. This may be a job on a building site where day in and day out they bust their arse for almost minimum wage, break their bodies to only find themselves drinking every afternoon to deal with the anxiety that comes from having to face that every day. Maybe they work in a remote mine in the middle of nowhere, they do not see their families for two weeks and then when they get home they are too tired to do anything. Maybe they have addiction problems, perhaps from a youth spent like most of us indulging in party drugs and now it's the only way they know how to deal with life and take the edge off. All of that predominantly affects men. All that torture, all of that hardship and yet no one cares. These are the men who eventually become sicker and sicker individuals until they do not resemble their former selves and end up locked up, homeless or dead.

Men choose to end their lives four times more than women do. Men's poor mental health is an epidemic in this country and around the world and I genuinely believe finding purpose, love and an outlet is a perfect way to save lives.

The truth is, to quote Henry Thoreau, "The mass of men lead lives of quiet desperation".

We are quiet

Why is he silent? Why isn't he talking?

You may think we are sitting on the lounge next to you thinking about all the problems in our relationship. Maybe you're worried there are other women on our minds or you're panicking that we are angry at you or we are stressed about something else entirely. You may try to fix it by asking what is wrong and we reply with "nothing". This confuses you because when you answer "nothing" to the same question it actually means "everything", but here is what is crazy about men: most of the time we are *literally thinking about nothing*.

Anytime you are worried that we are feeling anything, chances are you are completely wrong. You know the meme "what is he really thinking about?". It shows a woman imagining all the things her partner could be thinking about and it also shows the partner thinking about something completely ridiculous. The reason that meme is so popular is that it is true. Men will think and ruminate on some of the strangest things. We may be thinking about the last time our football team lost and or what they could have done to win, or maybe we are thinking about a better way to disembark a plane that doesn't leave everyone packed in like a tin of sardines. We may even be wondering why our ball sack has that line down the middle. I guarantee you we are not thinking about you or anything to do with you and I don't mean that in a "He doesn't care about you" way; men are just weird.

We also thrive on silence. It's not that we don't want to talk to you or communicate with you, in fact, it has nothing to do with you. We just love silence. It's a great place for us. We are happy, at peace and calm. This is where we think, sort out our daily problems and work out our future plans. Men may be bad at multi-tasking but mental multi-tasking is where we excel.

For some men a silent period is needed at a certain time. I'm interested to see if people relate to this. Many men need 20 minutes or so a day where they transition from out-in-the-world mode to family/with-their-partner mode. This may seem ridiculous but think about it; how many fights between couples happen the second someone returns home?

There are two versions of us and that is for good reason. When we are with our loved ones in the comfort of our own homes, we are relaxed, there are no outside threats and we can be the most genuine version of ourselves. When we are out in the wilderness, though, in a pub, around other men, we are always positioning among the pack to show our masculinity and display like a young lion, bull or even a ram in a way so as to not be seen as weak.

Perhaps this is why you'll see a different version of your male partner when he is around other men (this isn't an excuse to be an arsehole BTW). This spirited jostling is more common among people who are friends or deemed friendly. However, if we do not know the men we are surrounded by, we are always on high alert for violence. This is built directly into our DNA. After all, it's what kept our species thriving for the best part of half a million years.

It is an unfortunate fact that most violent people are men, so when we are away from where we feel safe and our group, pack or mob encounters another there is a chance, regardless of how small, that violence may transpire. We are not ourselves. This is why when a man comes home from work, he may need a few moments to collect himself and return to his genuine form. Some couples use this moment to argue and this is terrible. It'll result in the destruction of your relationship. Obviously this isn't an issue for all men but for most it's a reality. I don't need to take a moment when I get home. Why? I'm a genius and my ability to be an amazing husband has to be seen to be believed, but give everyone else a few moments and let them transition back into the person you love.

Women experience the same needs in going from one environment to another, so if you find yourself fighting with your spouse or partner, male or female, immediately when you or they get home, give yourself and them 15–20 minutes before you decide to recreate D-day in your kitchen. It may help.

We are very simple

Men are so simple it's borderline sad. Everything we do, like or have has a simple explanation behind it.

Why do we like cars? Goes *broom*.

Why do we like guns? Goes *boom*.

Why do we like violent sports? Goes *whack*.

Understand that and you understand men. It's really not that hard, ladies. Anything that makes you go, "ewghh, who would like that?", we fucking love! Honestly, if you have half a brain you can make your fella the happiest man on the planet with relative ease.

We're also simple when it comes to our sexual needs. For many women foreplay is a necessity. Maybe she wants to be wined and dined, maybe she wants to be deeply in love before she has sex, maybe she wants candles or lingerie. Here is something you should write down right now: men don't need any of that. Just be there, be willing, be nude, and *boom* we are good to go. In fact, we are always good to go, there isn't a moment where a man will turn you down. After dinner? Sure. Middle of the night? Righto. Haven't brushed your teeth? All good, me either. When it comes to sex our animalistic brain takes over. We were put on this planet to procreate and we will blow loads or die tryin'.

The same can be said for sexual attraction. Ask a man what is his type. Maybe he likes blondes or brunettes? Maybe he likes a great smile or a sense of humour? These are important for someone you may want to date or marry but when it comes to sex I'll be blunt: does she have a hole? Well, let's go! Men are basically dogs. We can eat the same thing every night, sleep anywhere, and stink but we love you unconditionally. All we think about is food, sleep and humping. It's that simple.

And the easiest way to understand your man, or any man, is to treat them like a dog. Sounds horrible but it's true. Pat us, love us, tell us we are a good boy and we will be content with life and everything in it. Did you buy us treats? Fucking oath, I don't give a shit about work or finances now, we have treats.

I'll end the dog analogy there and fair warning, don't do this to your dog, but the odd handjob goes pretty far by the way. We get the same happiness from a quick handy that you would with a $10,000 Birkin bag, so come on, ladies, have a go, will ya.

You'll never understand our friends

Ladies, let's face facts here; we have some weird mates. We have ones who are alcoholics or drug addicts or both. The ones always getting into fights, the ones always cheating on their partner, the loud ones, the rude ones. And we have no idea why we are friends with any of them. It sort of just happens. Asking a man how they became friends with someone is like asking an ant where they found that food they are carrying back to their nest. "I dunno, I just stumbled across it."

It must be hard for women to make friends. There are so many intricate moving parts. You have to like the same skin care, movie genre, type of music, TV shows, yadda yadda yadda. For men, we do not give a fuck. If we are around someone long enough we are best friends. We do dumb shit with our friends too, not to impress them, it's just what we do. If we are with enough of our mates with enough alcohol someone will get injured. It's all just part of being the average man. You may ask your boyfriend or husband why he even likes (insert name of your partner's friend you hate the most). Chances are we don't; we've just been around them for so long that we just accept that they are here to stay.

I know that it's not just men who go out and cause a scene with their friends. Ladies, you're guilty of that as well. Nothing like a girl's night to get you loud, obnoxious and falling over in high heels. The thing is there is just something about a boy's night that you gals just can't live up to. For example, ladies, I'm sure none of your friends on a night out have snorted coke on a church's steps, nailed their genitals to wood, tried to fight ten Polynesian security guards, shat in a bush and wiped your arse with a sock, or gone home with a 2 just because it meant a free lift. I would imagine you gals don't do that.

Here is the thing, though. All men have mates who do this shit on a regular basis and that is why we remain friends with them. We thrive on funny stories. It's the reason pub time is a good time; it's the place to share these stories, it's the campfire, it's how we unwind. You may think your partner goes to the pub too much and that may very well be true and the worry of alcoholism is a valid concern, but if you think he is there to chat with girls, don't be ridiculous. He is there to talk all matter of shit with his mates and reminisce on all the dumb shit they have done over the years. It is therapy for men and as long as we don't abuse it, then there is nothing wrong with it. So ladies, yes your man's friends may suck but just know we are fully aware and we accept them for the pieces of shit they are and you should too.

We are scared

We are, it's true. Once we drop the bravado and you see us at our most raw, you will see nothing more than a little boy who doesn't know what the fuck to do and just wishes their dad would help them through this moment. This is obvious in childhood; a boy will literally stand there screaming "Daddy!" when he needs help. But when we get older, become men, and have families, we have to play the role of "the protector";

a role that most of us aren't ready for. We all have moments where we are metaphorically screaming for help from our fathers. This may be the reason so many young men without fathers end up living lives that anyone would dread. We have studied this and fatherless men are far more likely to end up homeless, become violent, drop out of school and battle with addiction.

In my life, my father was infallible, I looked up to no one else but him.

I knew if the house was broken into he would defend us with his life.

I knew he would do what it takes to put food on the table every night.

I knew he would deal with life's problems for me.

I knew he would deal with my problems for me.

I knew all of this until he almost died of a heart attack. It dawned on me that he is just as scared as the rest of us and even though I saw him as this god-like human who couldn't be defeated, he too, I'm sure, wished some days that his dad could just take over and look after him; tell him that it's all going to be okay.

Men have this fear because we are the first line of defence for our family. We are the ones to be sacrificed if the house is on fire, or the boat's sinking, or god forbid, there's a war to be fought; and we happily take on those roles. But are we ready? There is no school for this, no certificate; you are just thrust into the world and told to "do your best". That's where a good father comes into play but, as I said, many men sadly never have that.

But if you want to know what scares men the most, it is beyond doubt failure. Failure leaves us in a state of anxious horror. In the back of our minds we are like a duck, never quite as tranquil as we seem, feet paddling like crazy under the water. Regardless of how well things are going, our unavoidable disposition devastates our thought patterns. Even at our most optimistic, we're awash with this fear of failure, worrying what will happen when we are tested and if we'll pass that test. Once again it's the insidious "what ifs".

Rightly or wrongly, men have ingrained deeply into our souls that the buck stops with us, that we are responsible for the care of our families, and that we must be the ones to provide for them and keep them safe. In modern times of course this isn't a prerequisite to being the masculine man we all want to be. Trust me, any man who tells you they don't want to be masculine is lying to you and themselves. In years gone by, safety, sustenance and prosperity were up to the men. Not anymore, which is wonderful. Women can do almost everything a man can and vice versa. But I believe without a shadow of a doubt that the software version we currently run on as modern men is not yet — and hopefully never will be — updated to fit the expectations of modern society. That's just not a world men are designed for. We need to be needed, we want to be wanted and if we fail to take risks, sure, we may not fail, but our life feels like nothing but a failure. We must risk it all or face the consequences of an empty existence.

So we are scared that everything will go wrong and we won't be able to fix it, that our fathers can't help us and we can't save our families.

Of course, ladies, we never expect you to really understand us. We are different in that regard. You complain to your friends when they ask how your relationship is going that he just doesn't understand you, that he is a Taurus and you just don't mix. We, of course, when our friends ask how the relationship is going respond in kind with, "She has nice tits."

Aren't we just a charitable bunch?

We do this because we are painfully simple yet confusingly complex. We will tell you exactly how we feel. We will give you straight answers. We are usually surrounded by some like-minded men and then some other strange ones we have just known for a long time. We need meaning in our lives and sometimes we are quiet. We usually know what we want for dinner. But peel back a layer from us manly onions and you'll see the strange inner workings of our minds. We want to keep the lawn mowed, we want to be fit and, for some reason, we see ourselves as some kind of hero who could save the world from a deadly cosmic impact. What's more, and this is much more important, we want your happiness more than we want our own and we will give our lives for our families. That's not speaking figuratively; I would die for my family.

All of these thoughts are constantly raging through our minds and it's difficult for us to contain them. That is perhaps why we see so many broken men. We see men whom we view as evil, but they just couldn't control what it is to be a man. We see others controlled by substances, it's not entirely their fault, it's not fucking easy being a man, and we see more and more men every year end their lives because, once again, it's not fucking easy being a man.

We are told constantly that women are victimised by society, that the patriarchy is there and always will be there to hurt women, and that you can't achieve X, Y or Z as a woman because of men. These may be very valid opinions. I'll ask you this, though. Just consider when people say men have it tough too, it's not because they are sexist or because they are a bigot, and it's not because they hate women or they bash their wives — no. It's because they are accurate. The reason you as a woman don't understand men is because we don't understand ourselves. That's men, that's it, it's all you need to know.

Women, on the other hand, are far more difficult to understand, and that's fine too. And I'll tell you why. It's because gender is a social construct, men and women aren't real and this chapter didn't matter anyway, good day.

Chapter 13: **It's okay to be masculine**

SUGGESTING THAT it is okay to be masculine may be the most obvious thing of all time. Of course it's okay to be masculine, the same as it's okay to be feminine and, for that matter, anywhere in the middle. Be yourself. If you are not hurting anyone, you do you.

That is how the majority of us think, but if you spend some time online in certain echo chambers you will quickly find that being a masculine man is akin to being a Neo-Nazi; you are basically in the same fascist U-boat. I'm not being hyperbolic, that is how some people think. Worse, these people have power and influence over others. There is a real threat to being masculine, the natural state for a man. People want it feminised or eradicated. I'm here to tell you it is our duty to protect it.

I'll begin this conversation with this: "toxic masculinity"

is and isn't real. It is real in so far as men who are masculine can be toxic pieces of shit but it also isn't real for the simple reason that masculinity alone is not toxic. Yes, there may be certain people and groups that are toxic and spread toxic behaviour, but they aren't toxic *because* of masculinity.

The reason why the myth of "toxic masculinity" is consistently perpetuated is because people *want* to believe the social media preachers — in spite of evidence to the contrary. Many men and women are affected by cognitive dissonance to the point where changing their mind would be devastating to their very persona. They will always refuse to publicly announce or concede that, obviously, masculinity *isn't* toxic, and that it comes down to the individual.

In the same way, Muslims aren't terrorists, but some Muslims are.

Women aren't bad drivers, but some women are.

Not all priests are paedo— actually no, bad example.

My point, pure and simple is: masculinity isn't toxic, but some men are.

What if a woman were to display a trait you might consider part of "toxic masculinity"? What if she held in her emotions, was sexually aggressive, was promiscuous, or wasn't a "feminist ally" (yes, that's a real example of toxic masculinity apparently)? What if she was violent, or engaged in unhealthy behaviour, or was homophobic? Would she be labelled as a toxic man? Of course not. Would people say she was displaying toxic masculinity? How could she, she is a woman. People would somehow find a way to blame men, of that I have no doubt, but if she behaved in this way it's not called "toxic femininity" or toxic anything. It doesn't reflect all women, so why the fuck are men all painted with the same brush when one cocksucker acts like a piece of shit?

I'll take this one step further. This is how I think about all those whom, as a society, we should look down on; the sexist, the racist, the homophobic and the transphobic. I believe that all of those labels are bullshit and here is why. Most people who are genuinely racist are probably going to be sexist as well. On top of that, they'll likely have a touch of homophobia and I bet you they aren't a fan of trans people either. I'm not talking about the modern use of those words where anyone who tells a joke or disagrees with a progressive worldview is so labelled, I'm referencing the *actual* meaning of these words; pure hatred. Chances are if you are one of these words then you will be another and, in reality, you are just shit people. It doesn't stop there. These people probably hit their wife and kick their dog. I would say, with a high chance of probability that they display toxic male traits. So is it fair to judge *all* men based on this man who is undoubtedly a huge hunk of shit? Of course not.

If you misuse masculinity, then sure, it can be very toxic indeed. Masculinity, if used incorrectly, can manifest in many undesirable outcomes; anger, violence, hatred, pain or sorrow. All of these stem from deliberate or unintentional misuse. Unfortunately, this is unavoidable for the simple reason of what masculinity is. Masculinity is a tool and sometimes tools are misused and people get hurt. We can't blame the tool in these situations. The blame must be focused squarely on the individual and what happened to them to cause them to use the tool in the incorrect manner. It's similar to the saying "guns don't kill people, people kill people", meaning of course it's not the gun firing itself, nor is it the bullet pushing itself out of the barrel at 3000 feet per second, it's the human being who made the conscious decision to use that lethal force. The same can be said for masculinity; it can be used for evil, like a gun, but only if the individual in control decides to do so.

We know the definition of the word masculinity, but the meaning of the word is much broader. It's almost like an unspoken rule; you know what the rule is even though no one ever has had to tell you. You understand almost everything about it although you may not be able to define what it means. We all know what masculinity is even though no one has ever actually told us everything there is to know about it.

To me, masculinity is providing, caring and protecting your family and being the barrier between them and danger in the off chance something horrible happens. It's believing in those around you and helping them to become better versions of themselves. It's caring and helping those who cannot help or care for themselves. It's fixing what is broken. It's doing what needs to be done. It's holding the door open for anyone behind you. It's not being scared to open up about your problems. It's saving someone who needs saving. It's teaching those younger than you. It's doing the impossible. It's doing what's hard and it's doing what's right.

It is not violence, it's not actual misogyny, it's not bottling up emotions. That is bullshit. That is what your grandfather's generation did and fuck that, we have moved well past that garbage.

Over time, the unconscious definition of masculinity, as understood by the wider population, has been skewed toward the negative. Of course, this is the fault of some truly shit men. But the mainstream media, the government, social media, celebrities and the education system are also complicit. It's popular to view masculinity, and anyone who exhibits masculine traits, negatively. This then encourages young men to avoid being masculine, which is their natural homeostatic state, leaving us with a new generation of weak, confused, scared and unmotivated young men. These young men lose all their bearings. They are desperate and sad. Many people believe being masculine is genuinely harmful. To them I say this: would you attack a woman for being feminine? Would you shame her for displaying traits that are seen as feminine? No? Then shut the fuck up.

This is a war and we are in the thick of it. I know it sounds ridiculous to call it that, but search "toxic masculinity" online and you will find video after video and article after article explaining in great detail that every single problem in the world can be blamed on men. Financial problems, violence, and climate change are all because of men. Of all the problems that women face, toxic masculinity is at the helm. Any issues children go through, toxic masculinity is responsible. We have an army at the gates of what it is to be a man and they have already broken down the palisade.

Take a look at the casualties on the battlefield of identity politics. The theory that "toxic masculinity" is an evil weapon of mass destruction that must be destroyed is nothing more than a Trojan horse designed to sneak past our better judgement and attack the real target — the male gender. I know it sounds over-the-top. Not everyone thinks this way. What we are really talking about here is the ability of the vocal minorities in the West to blame men for everything in their life.

When the former prime minister of New Zealand quit, who was to blame? Men. Female athletes are not as strong, powerful or fast as their male counterparts and who is to blame? Men. Fat women? Men. Not enough female CEOs? Men. The individual who doesn't rise to the top through hard work and dedication isn't blamed. Sure, some men stand in the way, but not in the majority of cases. When an innocent woman was raped and murdered in Melbourne in 2018, the entire country was saddened and in shock that something so atrocious had happened. But who was blamed? Not the perpetrator, it was the fault of *all* men.

It is bad enough to be vilified for your gender and demonised for how those before you have acted. What makes it worse is that men aren't doing as well as you'd imagine. These days, women outperform men in many areas. Of course, we should celebrate that women are doing well, but men should not be the collateral damage. Females outperform males in all areas of schooling; maths, English, everything. In fact, in some subjects the boys on average are almost an entire year behind the girls, and this continues through to university. More women are being accepted into university and completing at a higher level than men. But still more men end up as CEOs, so who is to blame? Men!

This is the truth across the board; young women are

doing better than young boys. The only areas in which men are dominating include sport; suicide; incarceration; violent crime; dying at work; working away from home; homelessness; and not seeing their kids, to name a few. So why are men doing so poorly?

Men are standing still in this world, like stagnant water puddled in the footprints of progress. There are many reasons for this, but one that is rarely discussed is that we have a generation of young boys from 3 to 20 years of age being raised by society as the villain, as the problem, as what needs to be fixed. That is powerful. Some boys realise that it's bullshit and I hope that is you. If you are a young man reading this book, you are *not* the villain everyone alleges you are. For others, it breaks them, leading to a life of solitude and unhappiness. For others, who have been told their whole lives that they are the problem, well, they start to believe it and lean into that mindset. They become violent. They become toxic. I'm not going to suggest that the only reason men are struggling is because we cop the blame on many fronts, there are many reasons, many that can be remedied, others which are set in stone.

All men start their lives as innocent little creatures, a blank slate, a new beginning. We are moulded by our environment and those around us. Many boys are missing something important in those early stages and that is a positive masculine role model, a father figure, a dad. We all have fathers but that doesn't necessarily mean they are good role models. They may never have had any positive male influences themselves, so how are they to teach you?

I believe this is why so many people looking to improve

themselves are male. The people who listen to motivational speeches are almost always men. Does that mean women couldn't give a shit about themselves? Not at all, but it may mean more men than women feel disaffected, as if they are in a dark enough place and that it's time to make a change. They know deep within their own minds that they cannot go on like this. Another 60 years of this just isn't feasible. They understand it's time to fix themselves. It's time to become the person they have always wanted to be.

Without positive male role models, it has been shown time and time again that men develop poorly. You can only hope they become introspective enough to see they need help and want to make that change. Sadly, most don't.

If you don't have a positive masculine role model in the home you miss out on so much. You may not find one anywhere else. Look at the schooling life of a young man. Almost all of his teachers are likely to be female — there is a good argument suggesting that the entire schooling system is aimed at the more feminine among us. Boys can go their entire lives without one piece of education from an older man on how you can harness your masculinity to help you be a better person and thrive in the real world. Could this be why we see so many young boys fail, in school and in life?

If a young man comes from a broken home, or his father is a terrible version of masculinity, they are far more likely to end up in jail; commit domestic violence; commit suicide; do worse at school; make less money; and be unmotivated in life. This then continues through the generations. Like generational wealth, some people end up with a lot simply thanks to those who came before them. And some of these boys end up terrible people just because of the life their forebears set up for them.

People get angry when the connection between fatherlessness and broken boys is drawn, as if it is an attack on the mothers somehow. The truth is, it just isn't. Some boys are far better off with just their mothers than their deadbeat fathers, but they still need someone to teach them how to be a good man. Mum can do that up to a point, but the only other person who can really teach and lead by example is another man who is leading a positive and productive life.

Men are broken right now. They're wounded. And men in pain act like dogs. We may seem content and happy, but this is nothing other than stoicism. It's dangerous because by the time you start to see a man cracking under pressure, the wounds are much deeper and it may be too late to rescue him from himself.

Across the Western world 80 per cent of suicides are male. *Eighty per cent*, let that number sink in. Yet when it comes to gender inequality we focus on shit that either doesn't exist or doesn't matter, like the gender wage gap and jokes about women being violent. Sorry, ladies, there are more important things going on. Why are men killing themselves every fucking day? Can you guess? Masculinity is to blame. Men are lost because they can't be themselves. They feel like they have done something wrong and are unfairly targeted and then when they end it all, who is blamed? They are!

For most of our history, gender inequality was at plague-like proportions. Women couldn't vote, they were held hostage in their homes and their husbands owned them. But in the West that is just not the case anymore. You wouldn't know this if you spent time on social media. The way fourth-wave feminists express themselves, you'd swear women are being tortured by their male overlords to this day and there had been little to no progress.

I truly believe feminism has done amazing things for women. It was and is a necessary part of human social evolution. The hard pill to swallow for many modern feminists is this: in the same way you need your femininity, you demand it, and you thrive upon it, we men need our masculinity. When we are consistently denied access to it, when we are constantly told it's something "wrong" that needs to be "fixed", we become more and more lost and troubled.

Every day in Australia, nine people take their own lives. Seven of those are men. The majority are white men, which raises more questions than it answers. Yet no one seems to give a shit. I guarantee you that if the suicide rate was 80 per cent women, if the tables were turned which would be equally as horrible, we would have government investigations and protesters marching in the streets. But when it's men, we don't seem to care. Is that grotesque and perplexing? Is it because men have had it far too good for far too long? Even that statement is incorrect. *Some* men have had great opulence and been in wonderful positions of wealth and power but the vast majority of men throughout history have had nothing. My point is the war on men is a grave misjudgement. They aren't the enemy. They are suffering as much as anyone else, if not more.

This may shock you, but one great substitute for a positive male role model is contact sport. It sounds counter-intuitive, but by competing in contact sports, you learn so much about the human being you are and what you are capable of. The same can be said for women who compete, but for boys this should be a requirement of growing up. Young men, like any animal in the wild, go through a charge of testosterone during their adolescent years. And this is why expressing themselves through the controlled violence of a contact sport is so important. The two sports I took part in where I learnt the most about myself were rugby league and the martial art jiu-jitsu. I played rugby league for 17 years and trained in jiu-jitsu gyms for only a few years, but I'll never forget the lessons I learnt.

Jiu-jitsu taught me how to remain calm in the worst-case scenario when you "roll" (compete) on the mats. In jiu-jitsu you aim to go to the point of killing or permanently injuring your opponent but stopping just before you cross that threshold. When you find yourself in terrible positions, and it happens a lot when you begin, you panic and basically ensure your defeat. You must learn to control your breathing and think before you do anything. What a great lesson for life. You are going to face so many challenges, in many of which you may panic and lose the capacity to problem solve. If you find yourself in that situation in the real world — where your heart is racing and all seems lost but you must stay calm and think — you will be ready.

As for rugby league, I loved trying to hurt people. That

was my favourite part of the game. Ironically, my biggest fear was being hurt myself. One of my responsibilities in the position I played was running with the ball into the opposition's biggest players, all 100 kilogram men trying to inflict pain upon me. Sometimes I'd relish these runs, particularly from a kick-off where I could get a long run up and fly into them like a wrecking ball. This requires courage and quite a bit of stupidity. I didn't learn much from these runs — the best lessons came from the runs where my team was under pressure. Often we would face this when held down in our end of the field, running from our try line (end zone) trying to put a dent in the opposition. These runs were made all the harder because you were often exhausted. As the great NFL coach Vince Lombardi once said, "Fatigue makes cowards of us all." But every time I made the effort and completed those challenges I strengthened that part of my brain that told me even if it is hard and seems impossible, even if it is going to hurt, we are going to do it anyway.

I worry that with more and more kids not competing in these sports, for valid reasons like the risk of concussion, they will miss out on some very important life lessons. If young men don't learn these lessons through sport, they'll never be able to replicate the experience in the real world. This in turn will make life just a little harder for them. If you are worried about concussion from sports like rugby league, American football, boxing and MMA, then give jiu-jitsu a try. It's one of the only contact sports where you can train at 100 per cent and the risk of injury is minimal.

If you don't have these experiences in early life, if you're not taught these important life lessons, weakness will envelop the body and the mind. Of course it doesn't happen in every case and some young men who participate in contact sport still become poor examples of what it means to be a man, but nothing else in my first 20 years prepared me as well for the shit that life would throw my way. I feel a connection between other friends who had a similar introduction to self-imposed hardships. I feel I can trust them, and I feel safer with these kinds of men in areas where violence could erupt. I know these kinds of men will not back down from danger. Other men may run, they may flee, and those I can't trust. This isn't just in the physical sense either. Those men will run when business negotiations get tough, or when your house catches fire. It may seem hyperbolic, but a man needs to be surrounded by like-minded males, ready to go into battle for each other. The caveat is it can easily turn toxic. You must control the courage and the energy and only use it in an emergency. Those who cannot control it aren't real men; they are angry, violent and weak pieces of shit.

    I despise how quickly toxic masculinity has superseded any other notions of what it means to be a man. This label, I fear, has been set in stone and perhaps we may never be able to shake it. In our world right now all forms of masculinity — the good, the bad and the indifferent — are *all* seen as toxic. American preacher James Freeman Clarke in the late 1800s had a better term for it. He didn't refer to the negative sides of masculinity as "toxic masculinity", he called them "false manliness". I found one of his speeches on YouTube, read aloud by an actor. Clarke begins with the powerful line,

"A false notion of manliness leads boys astray."

I sat with that idea for some time and it made more sense to me than anything else I have ever heard or read on the topic of men or masculinity. We are all men trying to answer the questions: what is the meaning of life? And what is a real man? A definition is impossible to reach. There are so many versions of masculinity that to attempt to narrow it down to one simple meaning, much like answering the question of what is the meaning of life, is futile. We can turn to Greek philosophers, great historical figures or modern thinkers for their opinions, but we won't get any closer.

Masculinity is diverse. It's different for everyone and that's great. It doesn't need to be the simple 1's and 0's of the 1950s. We don't need to be like our grandfathers; we can be exactly who we are now and still be masculine. Our sexuality doesn't matter either. Nor do our jobs. What matters are our actions, what we do in our homes, what we do around friends and what we do alone in our minds. Masculinity is the current scapegoat for evil, but without it, to borrow an Australian expression, we would be fucked.

Masculinity is necessary. Storming the beaches of Normandy on D-Day, that was masculinity. The Spartans lead by Leonidas fighting to the death and living forever in legend, that's masculinity. It's not just war and carnage where masculinity dwells, it's a family that can sleep soundly at night, knowing their father will keep them safe.

When we censor our masculinity, when we crush it or hide it, we lose the ability to be who we actually are at a biological level. Women love to talk about their femininity and how empowered it makes them feel. Well, ladies, it's the same for us. This is who we are, this is how we are built and when you try to control it and change it, we become lost.

Young men are desperate. Young boys walking into high school this year have been told since kindergarten that there's something wrong with how they were born. They have been conditioned to think they are the problem. These are kids, they haven't done anything to anyone, how fucking dare you make them feel as if they should be ashamed because they have a dick between their legs. That's everything progressive people throughout history have fought against and yet here you are not just condoning it but enforcing it. This action, encouraged by social media, identity politics and the mainstream media is reprehensible. Mark my words, if this continues, the number of young men ending their lives will exceed the already alarming numbers we see today.

Young men and boys are lost, they are desperate, they have no meaning, they have no purpose, they are the pawns of humanity, and no one cares what happens to them. More importantly, we all know that, and it's not going to change, so it's time to employ an allegedly toxic masculine trait: stoicism. You as an individual must understand that no one is here to help you, no one will take your hand and guide you through life. You must be the one to do it for yourself and your family as well. What a burden to bear.

In a family the woman gives birth; it is one of her great sacrifices. She suffers pain, changes in her body, mental and physical scars; that's her burden. Yours, gentlemen, is knowing that life is tough. It is hard and no one gives a fuck about you (outside of your family, but even that's not guaranteed). The world isn't going to help you, it's going to suck, and you're going to struggle. If it comes to it, you must sacrifice your life for the ones you love, or even a stranger. You are expected to work your fingers to the bone, you can only stop when you take your last breath, you and only you are the one who must take all of this on. Accept it, stare life in the face and smile. *That* is how you survive.

Toxic masculinity is bullshit but don't for a second think that shit blokes don't exist. If that is you, change. You *can*. If you won't, then fuck off and return this book. I don't want your shitty money. You are part of the problem. Real men are the perfect combination of caged violence and feminine kindness. So be the best version of yourself, help those around you, and leave the people you encounter better for the experience of meeting your masculinity.

Chapter 14: **Do things you hate**

YOU KNOW that feeling of standing in a nice, hot shower on a freezing cold winter's morning before you go to work? You're comfortable. You're safe. The last thing you want to do is get out and take on another day in the world. You might think to yourself, *What if I just stayed here forever?* The same goes for lying in a warm bed at 6 in the morning on a Monday. The easiest thing to do, is to do nothing.

This feeling of comfort precedes everything and anything worth doing in life. The easiest option is just to do nothing, stay still, remain in bed or in the shower and this is the option most people choose. But why not try an ice-cold shower instead? Or how about a 6 am gym session? The first day sucks and to be honest so does the 100th, but each time you do it, each time you embrace that shit feeling and beat down the voices in our heads telling us no, everything else in your life becomes just that little bit easier.

The path of least resistance by definition makes us focus on comfort, but without pressure — and without pain — we never evolve, we never change and we never reach the heights we wish we could climb to. The best way to prepare yourself to do the impossible is to harden your metal, day after day. This goes for every person on this planet and there are many ways to do it.

Artificial stress

We all face stress. We're taught how to be stressed very early on in our lives. Take any eight-year-old kid who's just spent six hours at school learning and doing things they do not want to do. They'd much rather be out playing, running around or watching TV. They come home from school and what are they met with? Homework! This teaches children to carry the stress of the day — stuck at school where they really don't want to be — back home with them. Rather than experiencing the great relief of kicking off their shoes at the front door, they have to deal with more work that wasn't covered in that six-hour period at school.

This follows us through schooling, into work life, parenthood and retirement. We are so stressed we resemble antelope on the savannahs of Africa terrified of what will be stalking them next. Our bodies are constantly flooded with the stress hormone cortisol. Remain in this state for long enough and you're going to get really sick. Or die. Being stressed when you're eight years old may just be the start of a lifelong subconscious obsession that ends with you having a heart attack before your 60th birthday.

Unfortunately, it's already too late for most of us adults; we have been *programmed* to be stressed out of our brains. So how do we beat it? The answer is *artificial stress*.

Why do people love the gym?

Going to the gym releases endorphins, you achieve something, and you see progress, right? All of this is true, but I believe the real reason why so many people have to train on a daily basis to live and function is this: the time spent in the gym is so horrible, pushing weights is so hard, that every other thing you face that day pales in comparison. Running is the same. Running fucking sucks, but if you can run for 30 minutes, or an hour, or whatever evil time you set yourself, that battle you have in your mind trumps any stress you may encounter that day. Ditto ice baths and saunas, both of which are really fucking uncomfortable.

Of course there are health benefits, from a reduction in inflammation to releases of adrenaline and noradrenaline. They also increase your metabolism, boost your mental health, and improve your focus and awareness more than drinking 20 coffees. But what an ice bath and a sauna also do, in similar, but different ways to exercise, is *train the mind*. I went to saunas throughout my twenties, but only started taking ice baths in early 2023. The horror that you face when your skin is boiling or you are up to your neck in frozen water is like nothing else. You are as close as you can safely get to death; a few more minutes in this bath or in this sauna, you may lose all function in your hands and feet and lose the ability to get out! (Side note: do it safely!) When you sit in frozen water, and decide that you're going to stay there for two, three or five minutes, your breathing and the pain is all you can think about. Nothing else matters. Your body's fight or flight response is in full swing and it is screaming at you to get the fuck out. But if you can calm that voice, face that demon, sit with the pain and be calm with the stress, then all else that headhunts you that day will be a walk in the park.

Do jobs that suck

I've had so many jobs I cannot for the life of me remember them all. The days of leaving school and working in the same place until you retire have gone the way of lead paint, asbestos and no sex before marriage. Our grandfathers may have worked at the same factory or office, doing the same job with the same people for 40+ years, but that's very rare these days. What a monotonous life it must have been. From the age of 14 or so they'd turn up at 6 am to start work then come home and repeat the routine ad nauseam. No wonder relationships with their wives and children often sucked.

I've argued with people about this before but I genuinely believe that from the age of 16 up until your thirties you should work in any and every position you can possibly find. I worked in restaurants, bars, security, landscaping, installing shower screens, marketing, door-to-door sales, youth work, disability care, and as a pizza delivery driver (great job but dangerous for dudes who love pizza).

I learnt so much from all of these gigs; usually that I didn't want to do them for the rest of my life and would do anything I could to avoid that. My first full-time job out of school was a great example of how I came to motivate myself to find something better. In March 2013, I had just come off months of drinking and enjoying my first summer out of school with my mates. I ended up with a university admissions score of 64 — which when you consider it's out of 100 is pretty shit — but here I am writing a book so stick that up your arse, teacher people. The truth is, I was just never motivated or took much interest in the school curriculum. The same could be said for university. The only chance people with my personality have of really educating themselves and doing well is undertaking that learning later in life.

Instead of trying to do a bridging course at university, I started work as a storeman; that's the guy who receives the stock, puts it away, then receives orders and sends them out. Possibly the most boring job of all time. Nothing was stimulating, nothing was interesting and the days dragged on and on. A year went by and I came to the realisation that this wasn't me, this wasn't what I wanted. All I was doing was desperately waiting for the work week to finish so I could go to the pub. While that's fun for a bit, I quickly realised I was headed the way of our grandfathers: stuck in the same job for life. And that just wasn't how I wanted things to go.

I decided to make a change and that's when I found myself one of the best jobs I ever had. At the age of 19 I started working at a pub in Newcastle. I was surrounded by mates, it was a very cruisy job and after every shift, you had a few beers. What more could a young bloke ask for?

One Anzac Day, one of the biggest days of the year where people are drinking from 8 am, we had some blokes join the security detail from the Cross in Sydney. For those who don't know, Kings Cross is the Las Vegas of Australia, except on a much smaller scale and a fucking dive, but the security guards were the real deal. Every Anzac Day without fail, fights would break out in the afternoon. Sure enough, on this particular day a brawl kicked off, spilling out onto the road. I saw it happening and saw all the other security guys running, so I joined in.

I'd never been in a fight in my life, I didn't know what the fuck I was doing, but I was on my way. I separated one guy from another, basically bear hugging him to stop the fight, but then out of nowhere, this skinny little shit took a swing at me. He missed with his fist but collected me with his forearm. That's when one of the huge bouncers came over and grabbed this little fuck so he couldn't move. I took him by the back of the neck and squeezed as hard as I could — I didn't know what else to do. The bouncer looked me in the eye and said, plain as day, "Uppercut him, bra. I got him. Smash him!"

I didn't, by the way. I just sort of stood awkwardly and then walked away. Afterwards, the bouncer came over and asked me if I was okay. "You could of fucking fucked him up, cuz," he said.

It was at this point I knew this might not be the career for me.

It was a shame because I loved working at that pub. It was super relaxed, except for fights. I worked security and behind the bar, checking IDs, pouring beers and collecting glasses in between talking shit with the locals. One night I was standing out the front making sure the patrons arriving were over the age of 18. This was a strange part of my job as it's a bit of a power trip. I only ever liked checking the IDs of guys who walked in like they had 10-foot dicks, just to bring them back to earth. Anyway, the sun was setting over the lake the pub looked onto and out of nowhere an old Commodore ripped into the carpark at a speed only pensioners with nothing left to live for and looking to take a few people with them to the afterlife drive. The car hit the wedge of concrete put there to stop lunatics and old people from flying into the pub and screeched to a stop.

Out of this old, beat-up Commodore emerged a giant. Huge. Bigger than me and I'm six foot eight. A bald, angry-looking guy. Whenever I was faced with situations like this, whenever I knew someone was going to cause trouble, I'd always try to become friendly with them. The thinking being, you are less likely to get punched in the face or stabbed by someone if you'd recently had a bit of a laugh with them.

This guy walked up to the front doors of the pub. I had a bit of a chat with him, exchanged pleasantries and he entered. Seconds later I got a phone call from my boss, who was inside the pub somewhere. It turned out he'd just watched the big fella walk in on the CCTV cameras. He told me to come to his office. I found him sitting with a huge smile on his face. "Do you know who that bloke is?" he asked me. I had no idea. But my boss did. The giant, terrifying dude had just got out of jail after a lengthy sentence for murdering someone. On top of that, my boss told me with an even bigger smile, "He loves young guys." Fuck. I was 19. My anxious mind was immediately flooded with the idea that this murderer probably wanted to make sweet jail love to me — before killing me.

It wasn't pure paranoia. Sure enough, when I went back out to the main area of the pub, the big bear started following me around. He started asking me questions. Do you work out? Where do you live? Is your family from around here? Now maybe he was just being polite, maybe. But then he started dancing. He noticed me watching him and he winked at me.

I wish I could tell you that was the end of the story, I wish I could, but I can't. Of course old mate started carrying on, spilling drinks and being aggressive. He was displaying all of the tell-tale signs of an intoxicated person who needed to be ejected from the venue. This was the part of the job I enjoyed the least. I was getting paid $20 an hour, nowhere near enough to get punched in the face. I was used to threatening people and receiving threats — you may be surprised to learn everyone in Newcastle used to be a pro boxer, or so I was told on almost every single shift — but there was just something about this guy. So for the very first time, I said to myself, *Nup. I'm not kicking him out. This is a job for the boss.*

The boss, whom I'm still friends with to this day, was a very imposing figure. I'd seen him staunch hundreds of people. He looked like a younger version of Ron Perlman who played

Clay in *Sons of Anarchy*. I knew everything would be absolutely fine with him at the helm, and it was. The terrifying dude had a bit of an argument but got in his car, blind drunk and sped off; nearly taking out a few cars in the process.

One of the pub's neighbours had seen the commotion the giant had caused and decided to call the police. The coppers pulled him over a few kilometres down the road. They searched his car and found a sawn-off shotgun, a machete, a handgun, and ammunition. I think they also found duct tape in the boot, but maybe that's just a good story getting in the way of the truth. I do know that the police later searched his home because of his parole breach, and there they found more guns and the house wired with explosives.

The following day I told my boss in the nicest way possible that he could stick his $20 an hour up his arse. I told him I was done dealing with blokes trying to kill me — or fuck me. Sure, I was scared of being shot, but I was more scared of the sexual threat. It's the only time I felt vulnerable in that kind of situation, and I empathise with women who feel like that every day. It's fucking horrible.

If I never chopped and changed jobs and just settled, got married young, got myself a mortgage and a few kids, then I probably would have become stuck doing the same old shit for the rest of my existence. Maybe you're doing this right now and maybe you're offended that I called it "shit", but let me ask you this: did you ever imagine when you were young working in the job you are now? I bet you wanted to do all these amazing things and yet you stopped trying.

I know so many people in the comedy industry who have

never had a real job. They don't work hard enough because they don't know what's on the other side. You see Instagram creators, YouTube creators, and TikTok creators whinging about burnout. Shut the fuck up and realise how most people live their lives, you fucking twats. Most people — both men and women — lead lives of "quiet desperation". But it doesn't have to be that way. Quit jobs you hate, keep looking and you never know who you will meet or what you will learn along the way. It's hard to let go of a solid stream of income to focus on a dream or a passion, but taking that risk separates those who stay at the same job for their entire life then retire sad, and those who really fucking squeeze the lemon. So change jobs, change careers. Don't make life decisions based on how much debt you are going to be in when you're 19, you idiot. Grow up a bit, travel, learn to love and then make these decisions. Otherwise you may live to regret it.

Prepare to fuck up

Everybody fucks up, but not everybody comes back from that fuck up. You must at some point ask yourself the question: is whatever I'm doing worth the potential fuck up?

It's like when you're gambling. The good gamblers only gamble what they can afford to lose. For some that may be $5. For others it's $50,000 (and for some cunts it's a lot more). As long as you are able to deal with the potential loss and the horror that may come with that, then risk it. If you aren't prepared for it, then play it safe. Unless, that is, the reward is so worthwhile that you would always regret it if you didn't at least try. Then and only then, should you gamble it all.

Some people are so scared to fuck up that they dare not even attempt things that may result in failure. I'm not sure where this fear comes from; it may be their upbringing, their DNA or maybe their parents' own failures, but many of us prepare from a young age to play life safe. You can see this tendency in some children; their adventure gene just isn't switched on. Some kids will run into the wilderness with wild ideas of what they will experience, others will cling to Mummy or Daddy. It's safe, but you never see the things worth seeing or have life-changing experiences. The kids who hold on for dear life to their parents' legs find it incredibly hard to let go. Have you ever tried to pry a child away from something they desperately want? Their faces red, they grip whatever it is they're terrified of letting go of with white knuckles, and it is this safety mechanism that will be deployed throughout their entire lives unless they somehow break the chain.

Of course, there's nothing inherently wrong with playing it safe. You can be happy, have a wife, a house, some kids, retire and die. But given you're only going to be on this earth for a very short period of time, a maximum of 100 years, wouldn't you rather take a few risks?

Risks have different meanings for different people. Changing jobs is a risk. Furthering your education is a risk, and you better believe following your dreams is a risk. These are all risks we recognise and understand. There are also risks that carry much greater consequences, like ending a relationship if you are not happy, leaving toxic people behind, and healing yourself after trauma. All of these actions can result in consequences both negative and positive. But are you willing to take that risk?

I couldn't think of anything worse than that image we all have in our heads of an old man or woman lying on their deathbeds recounting everything they wish they'd done if only they had their time again. Well, you don't get a second chance, so the first time you see a golden opportunity grab it with both hands and fucking run with it.

The problem with taking risks is every now and then you're going to fail. But much like when you're exercising, the greatest benefit comes from when you are working the hardest. It comes when failure is so close you can almost touch it. Relish that opportunity to grow, arm yourself with the lessons it teaches you, and prepare to come back bigger and better than ever. Most of all, be prepared to never allow it to happen to you again.

As you get older you will see so many people you once knew, whether from school or work, who never seem to change. It's like time has continued but they have remained motionless. You'll go to a reunion or your local pub when you're in your forties and they'll ask questions about your life. You'll tell great tales of triumph and tragedy, but when it's their turn to fill you in on what they've been doing, you could almost guess the responses. They hate their partner, hate their job, don't like their kids and their favourite thing is drinking because the only way to make their reality worth living is to alter their consciousness. These people are everywhere. Every group of friends has them. Do not let this become you!

The best way to avoid becoming one of these people is to allow failure to creep ever so close to you, maybe even let it in a few times, but never let it defeat you. Demand better of yourself and always be prepared to fuck up.

You're tougher than you know

My dad told me from a very young age that your mind will always give up before your body does. The moment your brain senses something is difficult it will always tell you to stop. In almost all situations, be that running, studying or meditating, if your brain decides it is too difficult it will tell you to quit. It's a protection mechanism and you will always have it. It has kept you safe in hundreds of situations before, and will many more times in the future. It acts almost like a guardian, reminding you that maybe what you are doing isn't such a great idea.

What matters here is tolerance and willpower. The more you can ignore the messages telling you to stop, the quieter they become, or at the very least it takes longer for them to appear.

I fight with these voices in my head all the time (which may be the most insane thing I've ever written). When I'm doing something difficult, say, running long distances, or facing another set of heavy squats, I have to literally argue with the entity that lives in my head trying to keep me on the path of least resistance. I speak to it like it is standing over me, like it wants to keep me down. I look at it like the weakest, safest version of me expressing itself. As I have continued this practice,

I've have always been shocked at what I am able to do.

The human body is honestly unbelievable. The fact that we stop trying after brief moments of strain when we can last days is incomprehensible. Running seems to be the most relatable example of this mental toughness (or weakness) because we can all relate to that negative voice telling us to quit. Some people run one hill and their brain isn't just telling them to quit, it is demanding it. It's making you feel like death is sprinting up behind you ready to end it all. You can't continue, you *won't* continue. Stop right now, your body is shutting down! "I'm going to die!" The reality, however, is humans can do this for days, for hundreds of miles. Ultramarathon runners do this all the time and yet your brain is telling you to stop after a few minutes. Who is lying to whom?

Of course, people who run for days, like ultramarathon runners, have years of training behind them, so naturally they can achieve much more than the average person. Well, yes and no. Sure, training helps but they were once the same as you, they just made a decision to stop listening to that voice in their head telling them to quit and they kept fucking going. Do that for long enough and all of a sudden you're running 100 kilometres for some fucked-up reason.

We often only relate mental toughness and defeating those inner voices to physical endeavours, but you can program your mind to continue and overcome anything that's holding you back in life. Your relationship, your job, painting your fucking house, it doesn't matter. If you listen to the voices in your head you will fail but if you ignore them, chances are you won't. It's that simple; just fucking ignore them and press on.

Doing things you hate and doing them consistently creates a more well-rounded version of yourself. You become battle-hardened, which in turn allows you to push past the difficult moments in life trying to block you from reaching the greatest heights. The greatest threat to our success in whatever we choose is us. We are the ones holding ourselves back. If we look back at every decision we regretted, or at every moment we gave up, chances are there wasn't someone standing there with a gun to our head forcing us to fail. It was just us.

We are taught from toddlerhood that "practise makes perfect" and the same can be said for creating a mind that is impregnable to negative self-talk. Unfortunately this isn't something we are taught in schools and unless you have parents who have achieved greatness or come up against great struggles, they're probably of little help too.

I am by no means an expert on any of this. I battle like a priest performing an exorcism with these inner demons every single day. They tell me not to train today because "I'm too sore", not to do the ice bath and to "do it tomorrow" because it's cold out, and not to write today and "have a day off" instead. The only way I have found to come out on top, is to set a standard of what you will do and then refuse to take a backwards step. Demand the best from yourself and accept nothing less.

So do something hard every day, especially in your youth, you'll never forget it . . .

ISAAC BUTTERFIELD is a comedian renowned for his razor sharp wit and unapologetic humour. Rising to fame through his YouTube channel, Butterfield tackles controversial topics with a unique blend of satire and insight. His comedy often delves into social commentary, touching on issues like politics, masculinity, and modern culture.

https://www.youtube.com/@IsaacButterfield

MY SIMPLE WORKOUT

Day 1: Chest Shoulders Triceps
- Chest Machine fly 4 × 12
- Dumbell Bench Press 3 × 8-10
- Shoulder press 3 × 8-10
- Rear delt fly 4 × 12
- Lateral raise 4 × 10
- Tricep push down (Bar) 3 × 12 - 15

Day 2: Back & Biceps
- Lat pull down 4 × 10
- Chest supported row 3 × 8-10
- Face Pull 3 × 15
- Standing bicep Curl 3 × 10
- Hammer curl 3 × 10

Day 3: Legs
- Seated hamstring curl 3 × 8-10
- Barbell Squat 3 × 10
- Lunge 3 × 10
- Calf raise 3 × 12-15

Day 4 - Rest Day

Repeat

(If you don't know how to do something, search how on YouTube)